WHAT WOULD OUR KŪPUNA DO?

AND WHAT WE CAN DO FOR FUTURE GENERATIONS

By Richard Ha
with Leslie Lang

What Would Our Kūpuna Do?

Published by Richard Ha, 2022
Hilo, Hawai'i

Graphic Design by Nelson Makua
Na Makua Original Hawaiian Designs
Puna, Hawai'i

Table of Contents

Acknowledgments

My Pop had no idea how much he influenced me while I was growing up. He was just telling me what he thought I should know.

I never gave a single thought to where he gained all his wisdom until recently when I started studying with Kekuhi Keali'ikanaka'ole's Hālau 'Ōhi'a. Then it hit me like a ton of bricks:

It was Hawaiian knowledge that his own kūpuna passed down to him, just as he passed it down to me.

Pop, this book is for you. It's also for the ones still to come.

Preface

In the beginning, all the energy we needed to produce our food came from the sun. The mastodons ate leaves that the sun nourished, the saber-toothed tiger ate the mastodon, and we ate the tiger and everything else.

The earth's population was limited by the amount of food we could gather or catch. Sometimes, the food caught and ate us. As a result, there were only so many people roaming around.

Then some of us started using horses and mules to help us grow food. It wasn't only the sun anymore; animals were providing some of the energy needed to cultivate food. Because that let us produce more food, there were more of us.

And then, about 150 years ago, we discovered oil.

Oil gave us the equivalent of millions of horsepower to grow food—and we didn't even need horses. The oil was plentiful and cheap, costing only about $3 for a barrel of it. We started using oil for packaging, transportation, and to manufacture fertilizer and chemicals to grow more food.

Food became very, very plentiful. We harvested and hunted for our food at grocery stores, and that worked well. The food didn't eat us. The number of people on Earth increased enormously. Life was good.

But it turns out that oil won't be available forever, and neither will the lifestyle we've built up around it—unless we make the right decisions today.

When our oil supplies are no longer available, nearly everything about our lifestyle will change—and not for the better.

That is, unless we make some very smart decisions. And we can't wait until it's too late. We need to make changes now.

I've spent a lot of time thinking about all this, studying it, and trying to ensure a better future for our grandchildren and their grandchildren. I wrote this book to share some of what I've learned.

Part 1

The Background

In all the years I've spent studying energy and sustainability, the most important thing I've learned is that Hawaiians were right the whole time.

Look at the *Kumulipo*, which is Hawaiians' two thousand–line origin chant. The *Kumulipo* was first written down in the late eighteenth century, but of course it's centuries older than that. The chant starts out talking about pō (great darkness) and goes on to describe the creation of the universe.

If you pay close attention, you realize its whole story is told in terms of ecology and physical science.

Pre-Western contact, Hawai'i's entire economy was based on energy and physical science, something we now call biophysical economics (a method of studying economy as it relates to energy).

Here's how the Biophysical Economics Institute defines biophysical economics:

> Biophysical economics is the study of the ways and means by which human societies procure and use energy and other biological and physical resources to produce, distribute, consume and exchange goods and services while generating various types of waste and environmental impacts. Biophysical economics builds on both social sciences and natural sciences to overcome some of the most fundamental limitations and blind spots of conventional economics. It makes it possible to understand some key requirements and conditions for economic growth, as well as related constraints and boundaries.

Though not in those terms, of course, that was the framework Hawaiians used to handle every detail of their economy and way of life. They also had cultural guardrails in place that ensured they managed their resources for the long run. It worked.

But then Captain Cook arrived in 1778, other Westerners followed, and it all changed. Land use, economics, and politics; literally, just about everything.

As the ways of life changed, here and elsewhere, people lost track of the fact that exponential growth on a finite planet is not sustainable.

And yet, the world keeps striving toward seemingly limitless growth. For example, more than 95 percent of the country's hydrogen, a clean technology that's a great energy resource for us going forward, is made using natural gas—even though natural gas is finite.

Here in Hawai'i, it's a different story. Here we can make hydrogen by running electricity through hot water from our geothermal source. Hawai'i sits over a "hot spot"—an area where heat comes from the subsurface of the earth—and will be over that spot for the next 1 to 2 million years. That geothermal resource will be available to us for all that time, for free. How lucky are we?

We also have the Thirty Meter Telescope (TMT), and have learned that Hawai'i is considered the best place on Earth to advance the science of exploring the skies. Wouldn't our navigator ancestors be proud of that? They were not only intelligent, but also curious. I can easily imagine them excited to learn more about a new frontier, just like they embraced learning everything they could about the ocean and what it contained.

Hawaiians already know how to manage their resources. They did it right for one thousand years. Now we just need to adapt what they always knew, and how they lived, to our current-day circumstances.

Chapter 1

How It All Started

In Hawai'i, we introduce ourselves by saying who we are, who our family is, and where we are from. It's Hawaiian style—tradition—and makes sense on an island where people want to place each other, find a connection, and know who they're dealing with.

So let me tell you who I am and where I come from:

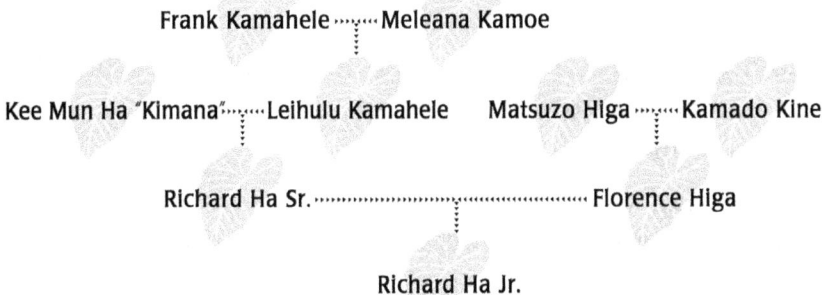

Frank Kamahele ⋯⋰⋯ Meleana Kamoe

Kee Mun Ha "Kimana" ⋯⋰⋯ Leihulu Kamahele   Matsuzo Higa ⋯⋰⋯ Kamado Kine

Richard Ha Sr. ⋯⋯⋯⋯⋯⋯⋯ Florence Higa

Richard Ha Jr.

MY PARENTS, GRANDPARENTS, AND GREAT-GRANDPARENTS

My parents

My mother, Florence Higa Ha, was born in Hawai'i to Okinawan parents. She was the rock of our family, the one who got up every morning, fed the chickens, and collected the eggs. I don't only mean that literally, though. She was the one who made everything happen.

My dad was the idea person, and my mom was the one who got stuff done. It's a good combination, and I was lucky to have them both.

My mom's mother, Kamado Kina, was born in Kitanakagusuku, Okinawa in 1899. She arrived in Honolulu in 1917, one of almost 20,000 Japanese, Okinawan, and Korean women who came to Hawai'i in the early twentieth century as "picture brides." Their marriages to immigrant workers in Hawai'i were arranged solely from photos and the recommendations of relatives back home.

On a November day in 1917, when my grandmother disembarked from the SS *Siberia Maru* and saw the man she was supposed to marry, she said no.

She stayed in Hawai'i, though, and it all worked out. She met Matsuzo Higa, who had been born in Okinawa in 1889 and emigrated to Hawai'i to work on a sugar plantation. They married and had nine children. My mom, Florence, was their third.

Mom grew up in Honolulu and then Moloka'i, where her father farmed. He grew watermelons and shipped them off by barge to sell in Honolulu.

As a young woman, my mom returned from Moloka'i to Honolulu, where she worked at her cousin's downtown café. Every morning, a young man who lived above the restaurant came down for breakfast. His name was Richard Ha (later, he would become Richard Ha, Sr.).

He and Mom got married in 1944. They had six children, and I was the oldest. Mom always said I was the one who got into most of the trouble.

I called my father "Pop." He was a good-looking guy with dark, wavy hair who stood about 5'6" and weighed 180 pounds when he was in fighting shape. He was a scrapper.

His ancestry was half-Korean and half-Hawaiian. But even though he was sometimes called Kōlea (the Hawaiian word for Korea or Korean), there was no question in anybody's mind about him being a Hawaiian man, not a Korean one. It's how he carried himself, how he talked, and how he thought.

My Hawaiian family is on his mother's side. Pop's mom was Okaleihuluokalani Kamahele (1906–1983), and her name was Leihulu. Leihulu's parents were Meleana Kamoe Kamahele (1882–1976) and Frank Kamahele (1887–1939).

Through my great-grandmother Meleana, I am the great-great-great-grandson of Kamahele Nui. In 1897, he signed the Kū'ē petition, protesting the U.S. annexation of Hawai'i. He was one of more than 21,000 of our Hawaiian ancestors who did so.

Life at Maku'u

My Kamahele family lived down the beach at Maku'u, between Hawaiian Paradise Park and Hawaiian Beaches, in lower Puna on the Big Island of Hawai'i. The family land, which consisted of more than twenty acres along the beach, let them be self-sufficient. The old house had rocks from the beach for its foundation. There was a redwood water tank and a Bull Durham tobacco bag over the kitchen faucet to filter the water.

With the ocean's bounty in front of the house and the taro patch, ulu trees, bananas, and pigpen out back, there was always plenty to eat. We were very poor, but we never knew it.

When we were small kids, we used to pile into Pop's blue '51 Chevy and head out to Maku'u to visit our extended Kamahele family. Just past the heart of Pahoa town, where Jan's Barbershop is today, Pop turned left and drove until we hit the old railroad tracks. Then he turned left and drove along the old railroad grade back toward Hilo.

The Maku'u railroad station was a few miles down the railroad grading. It was an old wooden shack with bench seats where passengers waited to ride the train into Hilo.

From there, a road wound along the expanse of pahoehoe lava and stretched all the way down the beach to Maku'u. That was before the Hawaiian Paradise Park and Hawaiian Beaches subdivisions were built, and cattle still grazed there. Someone from Shipman Ranch once said the reason there are a lot of mango trees at the center of the subdivision is because cowhands used to bring mangos in their lunch, and that's where they tossed the seeds.

We thought the Kamahele family compound was called Maku'u; we didn't know it was the name of the whole area. Our family's property ran along the ocean. There was a coconut grove, with fifty-foot trees standing thirty deep, running along the makai edge of the property. About half of the land was a kīpuka, an area the last lava flow hadn't covered that still had ten feet of soil. The other half, on the Hilo side, was pāhoehoe lava.

Our family home sat just behind the coconut grove at the edge of a slope. The house had green walls and a red roof. Instead of concrete blocks, big rocks from down the beach supported the posts.

Inside, lau hala mats four and five layers thick, woven of leaves from the hala trees that lined the road to the house, covered the floors. Rolls of the stripped and cleaned leaves, ready to be woven into new mats or to repair the existing ones, filled the house.

Everything was old-style—there was no electricity and no indoor plumbing. In the earlier years, there was a two-seater outhouse. And there was no phone, so when we showed up, it was unannounced, and our family always saw it as a special occasion.

We kids never, ever got as welcome a reception anywhere as when we arrived to see our relatives at Maku'u.

The person who was always happiest to see us small kids was my great-grandmother, Tutu Lady Meleana. She was tiny, probably one hundred pounds at the most, and gentle, but she was definitely the matriarch.

She spoke very little English, and I spoke little Hawaiian. I never gave it a second thought, but today when I think about it, I'm not exactly sure how we communicated. It was never an issue, though. I guess we kids knew enough basic Hawaiian that we got along just fine.

We loved to go down to the beach at Maku'u, and sometimes we went with Tutu to catch 'ōhua (baby manini). She herded the fish into a net that had coconut leaves for handles. I don't recall how she dried the 'ōhua, but I remember sticking my hand into a jar to pull out and eat one at a time. It was 'ono.

She would always get a few 'opihi and hāukeuke, too. We kids spent a lot of time poking around, looking at this sea creature and that.

My cousin Danny Labasan, youngest son of Tutu's daughter Aunty Elizabeth, told me about one memorable time when he was about six years old. Tutu Meleana took them down to Waikulani Pond. It's not really a pond, although we all called it that. It's a place where large ocean waves break onto a protective ring of pāhoehoe, and then their small swells roll gently across what looks like a pond. You had to jump from rock to rock to get out to Waikulani, something that the bigger kids could do without a problem. The little kids liked to poke around in that shallow, protected cove and look at the sea life. Sometimes they saw puhi (eel).

So Tutu and Danny's mom took them down to Waikulani. The kids swam and fished, Aunty Elizabeth got a bunch of 'opihi, and Tutu gathered some hāukeuke. Tutu was showing the kids how to clean the fish right there on the rocks, just feet away from the ocean, when suddenly a puhi came flying up out of the water and grabbed hold of Tutu's arm.

Danny screamed until he hyperventilated. He said he never forgot seeing that snake-like creature attached to his Tutu's bicep. But he also remembers how calm she was. She took hold of the puhi's head, pushed it against her arm until its mouth opened, and then removed it from her arm. She cut off the head, patched up her arm, and they walked back to the house. It's quite a story. I come from strong people.

Years later, when I showed an interest in playing slack key, Pop gave me Tutu's old Martin guitar. She played it so much that her fingers wore indentations into the wood. I've had it fifty-eight years now, and I think it's the possession I've had the longest.

Learning from my Pop

The Korean came from Pop's father's side. Pop's father, Kee Mun Ha, was born in Korea and emigrated to Hawai'i. "Kimana" was the Hawaiianization of his Korean name, and I don't know if that's what he was called, but I know that, later, that's what people called my dad.

I never met my grandfather, and all I know about him is that one day he was there, and the next day he wasn't. He just disappeared one day, and that was it—nobody ever saw him again. They thought he may have gone fishing and drowned. I never heard anybody speculate that he ran away; I don't think they thought that.

My Pop only went to school until the fifth grade, but he was practical and very wise. He worked as a farmer, and he knew about so much more than just farming.

Most of what I needed to survive in this world I learned from Pop, and a lot of times, he delivered his lessons around the dinner table. He would tell stories with impossible problems and then tell us the solutions. I can remember being about ten years old and sitting at dinner, listening to Pop talk, when suddenly he pounded the table with his fist.

"Not, no can!!" he roared. He pounded the table again, and dishes bounced off the table and fell to the floor. "Can!!" he yelled, and he stabbed his finger in the air. Those words stayed with me all my life.

I don't know how many times I heard Pop say in Pidgin, "There are a thousand reasons why 'no can.' I only looking for the one reason why 'can.'" He was telling us to figure out a way. The message was to never give up.

He told us kids to always find three solutions for every problem and one more just in case.

He taught us so many lessons about how to live our lives, and we heard them over and over: No excuses. Even if it's impossible, it's not impossible. Plan in advance.

He taught us what some people call "street smarts" and others call common sense. When you have to pay someone to teach it to you, it's called "contingency planning." Whatever it's called, I learned it from a young age.

I remember my Pop leaning forward with a clenched fist and a mean face and growling at an imaginary person: "No mistake my kindness for weakness!" I learned that from him, too.

Pop believed in a gift economy, which is how Hawaiians operated in older times. It's different than a market economy. In a gift economy, you give without an explicit agreement of reward, and then at other times, you receive.

Lots of us still operate this way. Too many papayas all at once? We share with our neighbors. Later when they have extra fish, they bring some over.

He showed us how to operate between two worlds—that one and our modern one.

Sometimes Pop's dinner table stories were about taking on huge projects with enormous obstacles and impossible odds. He could figure out a way around any problem, and he taught us to do the same.

Once, he told us kids about the night he and a couple of friends went fishing for āholehole at the tip of a rocky point. That was at my Tutu Meleana's place down Maku'u. Back then, there weren't collapsible fishing poles, so they had long poles, two inches around, made of bamboo.

They stuck one of the bamboo poles in the rocks and hung a kerosene lantern on it. Then, looking out to the ocean, they suddenly saw white water coming straight toward them. An enormous wave was about to completely cover the rocky point where they were fishing.

"What you going do?" my Pop asked me. I had no idea.

He told me he climbed the bamboo pole, hand over hand, lifted up his legs, and let the water pass beneath him. His two friends, who didn't think as fast, were swept off the rocks. After the wave was gone, he dropped back down and, using the pole, fished his friends out of the water.

Before the white water arrived, he already knew what he would do. He didn't panic because he had a plan. He raised us to think that way, too.

What a story. It really captured my imagination. It made a big impact on a young kid.

I also remember Pop telling us to have a contingency plan for a big earthquake, although he didn't call it that. He told us, "If an earthquake comes that's so strong it knocks everybody down, what you going do? You jump in the air and do a half-turn. When you hit the ground, immediately jump back up again. Do two half-turns."

How come do a turn, I asked? "Because after two jumps, you see everything," he answered. I thought, "Yeah, that's right!" Contingency planning.

Imagine you're a small kid, and the ground is shaking hard. Everything is falling over, but you're in the air. You jump in the air twice and do a half-turn each time. You look around, and you see everything. You're not falling down. You're stable, and your mind is clear.

I didn't realize it was a metaphor until I was older. And much later, I realized it's the same as what people started calling the "forty-thousand-foot view" after Sputnik launched in 1957.

Stay calm and pay attention to what's going on around you—that's what Pop was teaching us. This type of knowledge gets passed down through the generations. Maybe Pop learned it from his own father.

Chapter 2

Being Prepared—and Pivoting

Remember that news photo of the teenage kid in the "Make America Great Again" cap who faced down the older Native American man? That was a bad situation. When I saw those pictures, I could tell that the old man was the only person thinking clearly.

It makes me think of my Pop's earthquake story. The teenagers were hurling insults, and the old Native American man must have said to himself, "Holy smokes, something's going on here, and it's going to get worse if I don't do something." It really could have gotten much worse.

The adults who were chaperoning those students saw what was going on. They should have said, "Get in the bus—let's go!" but they didn't. Instead, they let the kids yell and jump up and down and do their school cheers.

And then the old man borrowed a drum and started playing and singing a prayer song. People's attention turned to him instead of the kids causing all the trouble.

It's like the old man was the only one in the air, keeping a cool head. He was looking all around while everybody else was just reacting, although to things they weren't seeing clearly.

In my Pop's way of thinking, the Native American man was the only one who handled it right, kept a clear head, and saw the whole situation.

The kid was just a kid. I'm not saying he was wrong or racist. But I never would have let that boy and the old man get face-to-face like that. It was the fault of the teachers and parents who were chaperoning. They were the adults, the kūpuna, and the kūpuna responsibility is safety.

I also would never, ever have let myself get into a situation like that where someone snaps a picture of me facing down an old man. I would have pivoted.

That kid should have stepped to the side, so it didn't look like he was facing down his elder. He could have led the old man out of there and I would have given him so much credit.

It reminded me of the people protesting the TMT being sited on Mauna Kea. That decision went to the U.S. Supreme Court already. The process is over.

But the protestors took photos of their kids and the women standing out in front.

How shame. Is that the image you want people to have of Hawaiians? Sending the women and children out front?

When you're warriors, you stand in front.

That's not an image of Hawaiians I want to be shown all over the world.

There's another story my Pop told us that stuck with me, too, although I didn't really understand it at the time.

He said, "Say you're driving down the road, doing 55 mph, and suddenly a dog runs out in front of you. What you going do?

"It's going to happen fast," he added, "so you have to plan ahead of time what to do."

There's no time to look in your rearview mirror, he said. You can drift to the left, but only if no one is coming toward you, or to the right if there happens to be a shoulder. You can touch your brakes, but only so hard before you risk getting hit by the car behind you. "What you going do?" Pop asked again.

We didn't know.

"Press the gas and run 'em over," he told us.

I didn't understand that at the time, but I do now. Pop was saying that to avoid something even worse happening, sometimes you have to keep going and run over the dog.

Hard to do? Yeah, but life is hard. Sometimes you gotta make the call. You don't want to hesitate and end up hurting somebody else. He said it was okay if you hurt or killed yourself. But it wasn't okay to kill somebody else.

Pop's stories were lessons in being prepared for emergencies—and life. They taught me to visualize solutions to problems before they happened. I always go through "what-if" scenarios in my mind, so if a situation arises I already have several solutions worked out. Because of Pop's early training, that's second nature to me.

I can think of two times when it actually may have saved my life.

The first time was in Vietnam, in a rice paddy, when a sniper opened fire on us. We ran and jumped into a small depression next to a thatched hut. But when we hit the ground, we realized there were already three guys hiding there.

I knew we shouldn't all be in the same spot because one grenade could kill us all. So I grabbed my radio operator and told him, "Let's go." We ran a short distance for cover, bullets flying all around us.

Right as we hit the ground again, we heard a loud *whump!* A grenade detonated right in the depression we had just left.

Street smarts? Common sense? Whatever it was, Pop's lessons about visualizing solutions to potential problems helped me do the right thing when there was no time to stop and think.

The second time Pop's training saved me was in Texas. I was flying down a two-lane road, top down, doing 100 mph in my custom-painted '62 Corvette.

All of a sudden, there was a car coming toward me. It was passing another car, so suddenly there were three cars side by side on a road that was only wide enough for two. We were all moving very, very fast and we were about to hit each other head-on.

"What you going do?" Pop's words had trained me for this moment, and I knew exactly what to do. I wasn't even nervous. I immediately flipped my right blinker on and started sliding over. I communicated nonverbally, and I didn't give the other drivers any time to make the wrong move.

The three of us flew past each other, safely, with only inches to spare.

I looked in the rearview mirror and nodded to myself. I wasn't even nervous but just laughed at the timing. "Yep. 'At's how!"

Learning from Uncle Sonny

I was a student at Hilo High School, walking with a couple of buddies on Waianuenue Avenue near Kamehameha Avenue, where Cronies Bar & Grill is now, when I heard someone shout to us. It was my Uncle Sonny, who was up the block toward the Kaikodo building.

"Eh, Dicky Boy!"

It's hard to be rugged when somebody yells that at you, loud, from a block away, even if you're in the ninth grade and already smoking cigarettes. I cringed and looked around to see if any girls had heard.

Uncle Sonny was my Tutu Meleana's son and my grand-mother Leihulu's brother. He must have been in his thirties then. His name was Ulrich Kamahele. I have no idea where the name "Ulrich" came from.

He always had a big personality, spoke loudly, and swung his arms around a lot. Later, my wife June and my sister Lei told me they'd learned to always keep at least an arm's length away from him, even if it meant they had to walk backward or make a big circle around the yard. They were staying out of range of those swinging arms, so they weren't all bruised up by the end of the visit.

Uncle Sonny traveled the world as a merchant marine. When he returned to Maku'u, he went back to living a simple life. He lived in the red and green house with stones from down the beach under each pillar. There was a redwood water tank and a spring on one corner of the property. The dirt floors had lumber over them. He built beds on those floors and then, old-style, stacked five or six lau hala mats atop each bed instead of a mattress.

Uncle Sonny kept his lawn and the whole area immaculate, practically manicured. He mowed a good distance down the beach. It wasn't only work for him; a large part of it was quality of life.

He didn't have running water or electricity, but he knew what was going on in the world. He listened to his transistor radio, and there was always a foot-high stack of U.S. News & World Reports on the table next to the kerosene lantern, with the current issue on top. I remember him picking up his magazines at the Pāhoa post office.

I visited Uncle Sonny a lot and stayed for hours. Most of the time, he talked and I listened. Not only did I learn to be a good listener, but I also learned a lot about life.

Everyone knew that Uncle Sonny grew the sweetest watermelons, so much so that he didn't have to market them. They all sold by word of mouth. People came from miles around to buy them.

We talked a lot about how he grew his watermelons. He used a poison pump in a backpack to kill pests, and once he showed me how he knew the amount of "sticker" to "spreader" in the mixture was right. The instructions called for something like a half-teaspoon per gallon, but after he mixed it, he always double-checked it by testing with a blade of California grass. California grass has fine hair on its leaves, and water usually runs right off it—taking the herbicide along with it. So Uncle Sonny knew that if water spread on the blade instead of running off, the mixture was right.

I learned some important lessons from that. I learned that more is not always better or even necessary. I learned to read the instructions but then confirm things on the ground. It makes me think of the word "grounded."

Uncle Sonny also taught me that melon flies—an enemy of the watermelon—rest under a leaf at the height of the midday sun. That's why he planted a few corn plants along the outside border of his watermelon patch. He picked up a leaf to show me, and there they were. He understood fruit flies.

The standard response to fruit flies would be to spray the entire field, but Uncle Sonny pulled out his can of Raid and gave them a short burst right there on the corn plants that he'd planted for that purpose. His way was much cheaper, cleaner, and way more effective.

One day he told me he needed to open up a new plot of land because he could not stay at the same place for too long; he didn't want his plants to get a virus or a wilt of any sort.

Over the following days and weeks, I watched him use a sickle to cut grass in the new plot and pull it into a roll and then cart the grass out in a wheelbarrow. When he wasn't doing that, he would take a hoe and remove the roots of the grass because he knew that otherwise, it would grow back.

The other type of weeds there had broad leaves from dormant seeds that germinated and popped up. Uncle Sonny also removed those with a hoe, but only on dry days and without disturbing much soil. After a while, the seeds stopped germinating.

Uncle Sonny knew that certain weeds would continue regrowing if the roots weren't removed, while others grew from seed. I noticed that, after a while, there were hardly any weeds in his new plot, and I thought that was amazing.

The lessons I learned from Uncle Sonny? Know what your problem is. Also: no waste time.

My grandma Leihulu lived with us for several years when I was growing up in Waiākea Uka. She grew taro and made poi, and she did the same things as Uncle Sonny. She always had a stack of California grass smoldering, even when it was raining—they were weeds she'd removed the same way he did. It was second nature to her. It was just her lifestyle.

Whenever I see a plot of ground that's clean like that, it's obvious to me that someone did that with a hoe and that they know what they're doing.

As Uncle Sonny got older, he started using pesticides, but because they cost money, he was very, very careful with them. It kept him from having to go and hoe the weeds or pull out the seeds. It saved him a lot of time. A few years later, he started using Roundup.

When I started farming, we used heavy-duty, skull-and-crossbones types of poisons like paraquat. When we switched to Roundup, we didn't have to use those anymore. It made spraying herbicides so much safer.

Using a chemical like Roundup in conjunction with a 100-horsepower tractor lets you do a thousand times more work than a single human can do. It means you can produce so much more food. But now that herbicides kill everything, you start losing that knowledge; you don't have to know what the old guys knew.

When Uncle Sonny used herbicides, he always stuck the leaf into it and saw if it worked. If not, he'd add a little more. He followed the instructions, but he never relied on the instructions for the final result. He knew the formula, but he checked to make sure the result was what he wanted. It showed me that he knew what he was doing. He knew why that particular spreader was there and checked the proportions to be sure. Not that he doubted, but if he wanted it to work very well, he'd check it himself.

I've never seen anybody else—not one person—do that. But I think it was common knowledge among the old folks.

We are so far removed from our food now that we don't have much of a connection with why we do what we do. But we need the basic knowledge.

You've got to know why you're doing the things that you're doing.

Positive influence on young kids

Another Kamehele I learned from was my Pop's cousin Frank Kamahele, another of Aunty Elizabeth's sons. He was a jet pilot and later the manager of both the Hilo and Kona airports, which all came about solely because he stayed at Maku'u when he was a small kid.

Here's why I say that. About a mile down the coast from Tutu's house, toward Hawaiian Beaches, there's an island called Moku 'Ōpihi. During World War II, the military used that island for target practice with its small planes and Hellfires.

Their pilots flew out of Hilo. As they passed Maku'u, they always waved to the small kid who was so excited by the planes that he jumped up and down and waved at them. Some of them flew low and turned sideways before they smiled and waved at the little boy. Others wiggled their wings and buzzed the house.

That small kid was Frank Kamahele, and he knew he would be a pilot one day. He didn't know how it would happen, but he knew it would.

When he was going to Pahoa High School, a teacher newly arrived from Texas became the basketball coach. Frank loved basketball, and that coach helped him get a scholarship to the University of Hawai'i (UH) to play. At UH, he learned about the U.S. Air Force ROTC program, and he joined. After he graduated from college, he applied for and was accepted to flight school in Arizona.

He told me he felt like the luckiest person in the world.

Frank came from a very poor family where nobody went to college. If it hadn't been for the pilots flying overhead and inspiring him when he was a kid, and that kind, dedicated teacher from Texas, he probably would have become a career "cut cane man." He was good at cutting sugar cane, which paid about $200 a month. That was a good living in those days, but he thought being a pilot was a lot better.

Frank was always coolheaded. He told me about the worst thing that happened to him during his flying career.

It happened at Honolulu International Airport one day, just after he took off. He was piloting a KC135 refueling tanker, which is a flying bomb about the size of a Boeing 707. When he was only about 150 feet up in the air, an engine fell off.

The control tower radioed: "Do you realize you lost engine number 4?"

"Roger," Frank replied.

"I repeat—do you realize that you lost engine number 4?"

"Roger." That was the extent of Frank's conversation with the control tower. He shut off the engine and fuel, so the plane didn't catch fire.

It happened to be a routine annual check ride, so there was a U.S. Air Force inspector sitting in the jump seat. The plane was flying well on three engines, and except for the engine falling off, everything was going fine.

Once they stabilized at altitude, Frank requested permission to land and get another plane so he could finish his mission. He knew he needed to get his crew up in the air again to keep up everyone's confidence. He landed the plane uneventfully and asked the flight inspector if he wanted to go back up with them.

"No," the inspector told him. "I'm sure you'll do just fine." The inspection was over, and that inspector couldn't wait to get off that plane.

Following his U.S. Air Force career, Frank returned to the Big Island, where he flew a six-passenger tour plane. He told me he couldn't bear to keep doing that, though, because it was so boring and uneventful. So he got a job at Honolulu International Airport as an administrator. Then, when the position of managing the Hilo and Kona airports became available, he returned to Hilo and got the job. He did that for seventeen years.

Frank's stories make me think about how important it is to provide keiki (children) with opportunities and enrichment. You never know what will grab kids' attention, influence them, and change their entire lives for the better. I remembered this as I went through my career and still always think about how we are affecting and influencing lives on the Big Island.

Especially the keiki.

Education: Take 1

After high school, I applied to and started attending the University of Hawai'i at Mānoa. But there I was, a small-town Hilo boy suddenly in the "big city," and there were just too many places to go, people to see, and beers to drink. After about a year, I flunked out of school.

It was the era of Vietnam, and flunking out of school carried serious consequences. I was drafted.

I made the best of the situation by applying for the Army's officer candidate school and volunteered to go to Vietnam. Just like that, I found myself wandering through a Vietnamese jungle, part of a hundred-person infantry company.

People were shooting and getting shot. Life suddenly felt very real.

I realized there was no way for anyone to easily come and assist us if we needed help, but there also wasn't a moment to feel sorry for ourselves. It took every bit of effort, skill, and cleverness we had to fight and take care of each other. To survive.

Every single person in our company knew that leaving someone behind was not an option. We lived by the unwritten rule that "we all come back or nobody comes back," and no one felt an ounce of uncertainty about it.

I really respected that attitude of taking care of one other, and I've held onto it ever since. I added it to the lessons I learned from my Pop.

When I returned from Vietnam, I was a different person. I had direction. I re-enrolled at UH and decided to go into business. I majored in accounting. That second time around, I did a lot better.

That's when I began to realize it really wasn't all about me and my generation. It's about those who are yet to come—our children and grandchildren, and their grandchildren.

I learned that, too, from my Pop, and it's how I think, always. When I'm thinking about a problem and its solution, I always think about how it will impact us ten years down the line. I don't just look at the immediate fix. I think about how it will affect my grandchildren and their grandchildren.

One thing that's very clear to me now is that we must use every bit of our skill and cleverness to create the best environment possible for the next generations.

When I went back to school for accounting, it wasn't because I wanted to wear a green visor. What I wanted was to learn how to keep score.

That's where I learned about break-even analysis, which was the biggest thing that guided us in our business. We did a break-even analysis every week.

Most companies wait for their accountant to run a report every six weeks or whatever. But being on top of it weekly let us make small tweaks as we went. It allowed us to look five, ten, and twenty years down the line and keep making changes so we stayed on track. We never got into a bad situation because we always knew exactly how we were doing.

It's still how I look at the big picture. I tell students to go online and search "break-even analysis" because, to me, that's the single most important concept when you start in business.

It's still who I am and explains why I am so concerned about the future here on this island. It explains why I am working hard on topics of sustainability and energy solutions. It's not all about me. We all have to survive. That includes all of us and our grandkids and their grandkids, too. What are we creating and leaving for them?

Leaving them behind is not an option.

Chapter 3

Chickens and Bananas

By the time I graduated from Hilo High School, Pop had the largest poultry operation on the Big Island with 35,000 hens. When I graduated from UH Manoa in 1973 with an accounting degree, he asked if I'd come home and run the family chicken farm.

I agreed and moved back to Hilo.

After a few months on the chicken farm, I was asked to manage the Hilo Egg Producers Cooperative, located next to Hilo Lunch Shop on Kalanikoa Street, which supplied Hilo's supermarkets with fresh eggs.

We had about twenty-five acres of vacant land—and lots of chicken manure we could use for fertilizer—so I wondered what crops I could put in. I noticed the grocery stores were full of imported bananas with those little blue and yellow Chiquita labels.

Maybe we could grow bananas, I thought, and if we moved fast, we might gain significant market share. But I didn't have any money to put into bananas. All I had was a credit card with a $300 limit and a Toyota Land Cruiser. In retrospect, that was good because it meant I couldn't rush in and lose everything.

Pop's motto sprang to mind—"Not no can, CAN!"—and I found ways to be resourceful.

When I delivered eggs to supermarkets, I brought home their used banana boxes and stashed them under my parents' house.

I traded chicken manure to local farmers for banana planting material. I got some from Mr. Kudo on Haihai Street, some from Eric Mydell, and some from Mr. Ah Heen.

I also got some banana keiki from Uncle Sonny. The Hawaiian Paradise Park subdivision and its roads were built by then, so it was much easier to drive down to Maku'u. I was seeing Uncle Sonny quite often.

I planted some bananas and then kept expanding, a little bit at a time. I kept going, and eventually, we were the largest banana farm in the state.

We managed to survive in farming for more than thirty years by questioning everything, looking into the future, and forcing change.

But when I started out I was young and green and thinking big. With my accounting degree and lots of big ideas about cost-benefit volume analysis and market share, I contemplated putting in hundreds of acres of bananas.

Maybe Uncle Sonny would lease me 10 acres of his land at Maku'u, too, I pondered. Maybe I could grow 35,000 pounds of bananas per acre on those 10 acres. I scratched my chin. Maybe 300,000 pounds a year, actually, if I took turnaround space into account!

While I was having my grandiose ideas, Uncle Sonny was making a living on his ten acres. He had ten or twenty hills of watermelons with maybe four plants on each mound. His watermelons were of exceptional quality, consistently sweet, and people drove for many miles to buy them.

He earned enough working those ten acres to easily support himself and send money to his wife and son in the Philippines.

I was really interested in watching how he grew those watermelons. He used tender loving care, very close observation, quick appropriate reactions, and good old common sense. As my Pop always said, "If a farmer makes money, a farmer will farm." Uncle Sonny farmed at a scale that was appropriate for him, and it completely worked. Watching him gave me keen respect for small farmers.

Although he had a freshwater spring and ten acres of deep soil, Uncle Sonny operated with the barest minimum of inputs. Instead of setting up an irrigation infrastructure around a water pump, he decided to haul water if there were a drought. I couldn't disagree; after all, he was doing well enough to send money back to the Philippines and support a family there.

Here's how he kept track of when his watermelons would be ready. When one reached the size of a golf ball, he wrote the date on a wooden stake and stuck it in the ground. Then a certain number of days later, he harvested the melons.

It was simple but very effective. It's what led us to keep track of when to bag banana bunches. We harvested our bananas based on elapsed time—pretty much like Uncle Sonny did, and we used a different colored ribbon for each week. That made it easy to adjust for seasonality. For instance, because bananas stayed on the tree for two or three weeks longer in winter, we just added an additional ribbon for each week.

I think the most important thing I learned from Uncle Sonny is that your business is successful not when it's big, but when it supports your situation.

It's what I always look at when I visit a farm. Not how big it is or how much money it makes, but how it operates and whether it solves the problem it's trying to solve.

I'm lucky I got to spend a lot of time with and learn from my Uncle Sonny when I was younger. I got a great feel for his old-style way of making decisions, and he helped me develop a good eye for quality and performance. He always broke things down into their essential components. He kept his life simple, and he was good at what he did.

I learned so much from him, and I admired him very much.

Banana farming, local style

I started out in bananas with my brother. We started our banana farm at Waiākea Uka under the corporate name Ha Bros., Inc.

Because we didn't have money to clear the land, we marked rows for bananas by making lines through the California grass with my Land Cruiser. We're talking tall California grass, taller than the Land Cruiser, that has those tiny hairs that make you itchy.

We still had more muscle than money at that point, so we used sickles to clear the grass and then an 'ō'ō and posthole digger to plant the banana pulapula (seedlings). Mom and Pop, my three brothers, and I planted all the bananas.

I was still thinking about my accounting degree and dreaming of a large market share, so I wanted to plant bananas as fast as possible. The sickle and 'ō'ō let us add fifty plants per week. (Compare that to today, when an automatic planter takes only six seconds per plant.)

We were so new to banana growing that we thought we should start by planting the largest plants, because then we could harvest sooner and get bigger bunches. Some of the plants we selected already had their bunch halfway up the tree.

Nowadays, we know those bunches are not saleable. That's because a banana plant needs maximum undisturbed time to develop a large bunch. But back then, we didn't know any better.

I can't believe how much we didn't know. It's kind of humorous to look back at how we started out.

I also wanted to start another banana farm as a separate entity, so I started looking around for parcels. But that was around 1978, when land was scarce because the sugar plantations had most of the good plots.

I did find a sixty-acre parcel at Koa'e and ended up leasing there. Elvin and Kay Kamoku owned it along with Bill Kaina. Elvin was my Pop's old diving buddy, and at the time, he was the Big Island's fire chief. Bill Kaina was pastor of Kaumakapili Church and, later, Kawaiaha'o Church.

It took about forty minutes to get from Hilo to Koa'e. The Pahoa bypass road wasn't built yet, so we drove through the middle of Pahoa to get to work. Then we headed toward Kapoho, past Lava Tree State Park, and past old Kapoho town, which had already been covered by lava, to the four-way stop. There, we turned back toward Hilo on Beach Road. We passed the Lyman cinder cones, and then the pavement ended, and the road continued beneath tall mango trees.

The farm was about one hundred yards on the left. It had no soil at all because of the 1960 eruption that destroyed Kapoho town. Cinder had spewed out of a lava fountain more than a thousand feet high, and the prevailing winds had blown it across our parcel until it was a foot or more high.

I was still pretty new to farming at that point. I didn't know, for instance, that you needed soil to grow bananas.

A farmer had been growing papayas there because they grow well in cinder. He'd ripped deep rows through the pahoehoe lava with a D9 bulldozer, and then planted his papayas down the rows.

I didn't have money to do anything else, so Mom, Pop, and I just went ahead and planted our first crop of bananas in those papaya rows. Luckily, the ripped pahoehoe allowed the banana plant roots to reach deep enough that they found moisture.

Later, I hired others to help us plant and take care of the evolving farm. Our original banana crew consisted of Miles Kotaki, our farm manager Jerryl Mauhili, Jason, Jolan and Jocky Keahilihau, Puggy Nathaniel, Jolson Nakamura, and Bert Naihe. Most of them lived in Keaukaha and Pana'ewa.

We couldn't afford a tractor, so we used picks, shovels, and 'ō'ō bars to plant the bananas as deep down amidst the ripped slabs of pahoehoe as we could. Then we covered them with a mound of cinder. We filled buckets with fertilizer and walked down the rows, tossing it over the plants by hand.

When the bananas were ready, the guys harvested the bunches, carried them to the nearest road, and leaned them up against a banana plant. After the bunches were all harvested, they cut off the hands of bananas and laid them in two papaya bins we had on a flatbed trailer.

Clearly, we were still operating hand to mouth at that point, because one day the papaya bins got repossessed.

We didn't have anything to put the bananas in, but Jerryl decided we'd haul them anyway. They put a bed of banana leaves on the trailer and lined up hands of banana, one inside the other, from one end to the other. They set banana leaves atop them and then stacked a second layer of banana hands, and then a third and a fourth and on up until there were seven layers.

The first time they drove their unusual load through Pahoa town, everybody's head swiveled: "What was that?!"

Our routine was to take the trailer to our Waiākea Uka packing house at the end of our workday. Mom cut up the bananas and had them packed in boxes by 6:30 the next morning. She did that for months, or maybe even a whole year. I don't know how we could have done it without her help.

After a while, my brother-in-law Dennis Vierra helped us build a packing house. Until then, there was no shelter, no toilet, nothing. Just a lot of determination.

Dennis could build anything. He built us a structure where we could hang the bunches and then roll them by rail to an area where we cut off the hands and put them in a tank of water. The hands floated across the tank, where we cut them into clusters and packed them into banana boxes.

We all thought we'd hit the big time, but it turned out nobody really wanted our bananas on O'ahu.

Because we had more guts than brains, we sent several hundred boxes of bananas to someone on O'ahu we called Uncle Chow, although we weren't sure that was his real name. He went around Honolulu and sold our bananas off his flatbed truck for 10 cents a pound.

But he never sent us the money. I ended up writing it off as marketing and promotion.

His efforts, though, got the attention of Stanley Unten. Stan owned Hawaiian Banana Company, the main banana distributor on O'ahu. He called me, and we started shipping to him.

Our next purchase was a large cargo van to take bananas to the dock. And then mechanization started coming fast and furious. We bought a roller conveyor to help us load the cargo van. We also used it to unload banana boxes into a Young Brothers refrigerated container.

Then we bought a used forklift for $100, and we thought we'd really hit the big time. It had hard rubber tires, and every time the wheel that was missing some rubber hit the concrete, it made a loud clunk. The guys named it Fred Flintstone.

But it could move pallets of bananas, which meant we no longer had to carry them by hand. We all appreciated Fred Flintstone very much.

At the time, loading a trailer to the top with banana keiki that looked like 'ōhi'a logs made us feel very self-satisfied. Nowadays, you could carry the same number of small, tissue-cultured banana plants under one arm—and they would result in bigger bunches of bananas, too.

We started by planting two acres of bananas, a total of maybe 1,500 plants. Then, after we planted, we just let them grow. We worked for two or three hours a day, and then my brothers' friends would come over. That's where I got to be friends with Dane Silva, the lā'au lapa'au practitioner who studied under Papa Henry Auwae and has a PhD now.

We talked story, and then hit the punching bag or lifted weights for another few hours. Then, pau work.

We went on like that for a year, and then we started to harvest. We packed bananas in the recycled banana boxes I'd stored under the house.

But it turned out that customers prefer ripe bananas. So we put the hands of bananas on chicken wire and let them ripen in one of the empty chicken houses. Then we picked out the riper ones to put in boxes. It was unwieldy.

I knew that on the mainland people used some type of gas to ripen bananas. I had no idea what kind of gas, so I asked someone at Gaspro if she knew of a product that ripens bananas. The lady asked me, "You mean banana gas?"

I said, "Yes, banana gas," and took a cylinder with me.

We built a room out of plywood where we could contain the gas and treat the bananas. We were amazed to see them ripen uniformly in just a few days.

Our first customer was Food Fair Supermarket. When we delivered our first box, we took a photo with Mr. Eji Kaneshiro, the boss there, which felt like a big deal. When I was in charge of marketing fresh eggs, I never even got to talk to him. Now, with our bananas, I was moving up in the world.

For some reason, though, individual bananas sometimes fell off the hand. I was called down to Food Fair many times, where I always acted surprised and promised I would fix it. It went on like that for a long time, and I had to talk to Mr. Kaneshiro way too often. It was like getting called into the principal's office.

I learned that mainland banana companies used refrigeration to control ripening. Because we didn't have money for that, we bought a small air conditioner, and it worked. It was amazing. We were delivering maybe ten boxes a week to Food Fair, and they were perfect bananas. We were using cutting-edge technology and again we thought we had hit the big time.

But then one day, when we had hit peak production of about twenty-five boxes per week, I opened the door to our air-conditioned enclosure and smelled the unmistakable odor of overripe bananas. What happened?

The air conditioning unit had ice all over it. That's when I learned that ripening bananas give off a lot of heat and we had overtaxed the small air conditioner. It was a disaster—we lost all twenty-five boxes.

I applied for a loan to build a warehouse, and we built three ripening rooms with real refrigeration.

After that, we were in the banana business for real.

The power of Mom

From the very first day, my mom worked so hard and helped us so much. Out of all of us, Mom was always the hardest worker.

She was also an example. Some of us were marketers and talkers, but she was a doer. She is, hands down, the person most responsible for our success.

I've been very lucky that my wife June is like that, too. Without Mom and June, we wouldn't have anything.

In those early days, any time we needed help Mom was there. She didn't just put in eight hours. She put in twelve or fifteen or twenty hours—whatever it took. We worked seven days a week back then, and that went on for years. She always said her work was a labor of love.

During the day, Mom worked at our Waiākea Uka farm. At 6 p.m., when the regular workday was done, I drove there with a trailer load of bananas from my new Kapoho farm. She stayed on and packed those bananas for hours until the trailer was empty and ready to go back to Kapoho early the next morning. When I think about it now, I don't know when she slept.

Mom was still working at the farm from 7 to 11 a.m. in her eighties. At that point, she worked in the plant nursery, which wasn't as physical, and she always felt like she wasn't doing enough. She liked going in to work and getting some exercise, rather than sitting home and doing nothing. It kept her active and gave her something to do. It kept her young.

Over the years, I bought her exercise equipment. Exercise machines, weight-lifting equipment, bicycles. She used them. I used to joke that I gave her exercise equipment so she'd stay strong and keep working for us. Cheap labor! But, of course, it was never that. It was for her health.

Every morning, I picked her up at her house in Waiākea Uka, and as we drove to the farm, we talked story. I told her how the farm was going and what we were doing. She was my sounding board.

Every once in a while, I'd crack a joke and she'd bust up. Mom had a great sense of humor and loved to laugh. We laughed a lot. We both looked forward to those morning drives.

Largest banana farm in Hawai'i

By the early 1990s, we were farming 300 acres of bananas as Kea'au Bananas, and we had become the largest banana farm in the state.

And then in 1992, the Rainforest Alliance awarded us its first-ever "ECO-OK" certification, an award we first learned about from Lee West. She and her husband Steve West are agriculture consultants in Yuma, Arizona, who we have worked with on various banana projects.

The Rainforest Alliance is the world's first and largest third-party certifier of banana production methods, and its ECO-OK program changed the worldwide banana industry for the better. It provided stringent pesticide regulations, waste disposal, employee conditions, and environmental protection rules.

The large Central American banana plantations were resisting the idea of certification, and then there we were, a family-owned banana farm in Hawai'i, causing them grief.

There were also politics at play. While we were the first farm to qualify for certification, we were told it would be bad form for a banana farm outside Central America to get the first ECO-OK certification. So we had to wait until a Central American farm qualified so we could be certified at the same time.

I remember the day we were at the Ritz Carlton in Kona with Kate Heaton, who had come in from the Rainforest Alliance's New York office. She was in contact with the Costa Rica office, and we were waiting for official word that we could announce our certification. It was exciting!

At around that time, I got a call from a Chiquita Banana engineer from Costa Rica who knew we were about to be certified "ECO-OK." He called me from O'ahu while on a stopover. He was flying to the Philippines to help set up a high-elevation banana plantation there. Their objective was to lengthen the time to harvest so more complex tastes could develop, like we do here in Hawai'i and in Taiwan, about 20 and 23 degrees north of the equator. Compared to those at the equator, our bananas stay on the tree up to three weeks longer.

So there we were, the largest banana farm in Hawai'i and certified by the Rainforest Alliance. A Chiquita Banana engineer had consulted with me. We'd come a long way.

Chapter 4

Moving to Pepe'ekeo

Then the devastating and destructive banana bunch top virus started spreading in Kea'au, where our farm was. It could easily have taken out our entire crop, and I decided we needed to lessen our risk by starting another farm somewhere else.

But where?

We were advised to move to Waialua on O'ahu's North Shore because it was close to the major market, and we also looked at several places on the Big Island. Sugar plantations were closing down throughout the state, so, uncharacteristically, there were some large plots of land available. We had options.

It eventually came down to a choice between Waialua on O'ahu and Pepe'ekeo on the Big Island. Waialua had the benefit of proximity to the Honolulu market and a functioning, low-elevation well for water. Pepe'ekeo had abundant rainfall and adequate, though not perfect, sunlight.

John Cross, an executive at the agricultural company C. Brewer, let me use ten acres at Pepe'ekeo rent-free to test-grow bananas. Back then, none of us were sure if we could successfully farm bananas in the deep soil and heavy rainfall of the Hāmākua Coast. Although I had figured out how to grow bananas in the rocks of Kapoho and Kea'au, I had no experience with pulling a plow or getting stuck in the mud.

Back then, the standard way to plant bananas was with the "mat" system. The idea was to plant 250 plants per acre. Then, for every plant you harvested and chopped down, you let four plants grow up. That increased your numbers to one thousand plants per acre.

We decided, though, that we would plant 25 percent fewer plants on those ten rainy acres, so more sunlight would hit the ground. We also planted in straight lines and then mowed the grass that grew up between the rows, so our machine would get some traction instead of getting stuck in the mud.

So I mowed the grass and pulled a plow to mark rows. Then every weekend for several months, Mom—who was 71 then—June, Tracy, Kimo, and I, plus our grandkids Kapono and Kimberly, planted banana plants from our own tissue culture lab. We'd learned how to set up a tissue culture lab from UH Hilo Professor Mike Tanabe.

Kimo carried a bucket of lime and dropped a handful as a marker every so many steps. Tracy or June drove the truck, and our grandson Kapono, who was around six years old, sat in the back and dropped a plant by the lime marker. Then, using picks and shovels, the rest of us went behind and set the plants in the ground.

Even Kimberly, who was about three, had a pick. She dug holes wherever she wanted.

After all the plants were in the ground, we took buckets and fertilized them.

We expected a drop in production since we'd planted fewer plants, but we actually found that the bunch sizes were larger.

Banana farming at Pepe'ekeo was more efficient than we'd expected.

At the end of our test year, we felt it would work to grow bananas in Pepe'ekeo. So we had a small ceremony and Doc Buyers, who was C. Brewer's chairman of the board at the time, cut the first bunch of bananas. Other C. Brewer executives present were Jim Andrasick, who was president and, later, chairman of the board of Matson; Willy Tallett, senior vice president of real estate/corporate development; and John Cross, who later became president of Mauna Kea Agribusiness (the company that succeeded C. Brewer).

We had huge dreams, so we didn't feel at all awkward celebrating our measly ten acres in front of this group of heavy-duty corporate sorts who represented C. Brewer's tens of thousands of acres.

We knew where we were going, and it felt very appropriate that they were there.

So, with our test a success, we decided to move to the 600-acre Pepe'ekeo property. We'd proven there was enough sunshine, and we liked that there was so much free water on the land. In addition to all the rainfall, there were also three springs and three streams. Before we arrived, the sugar plantation that operated there was authorized to use six million gallons of water per day from those streams.

One large spring on our property had, in the past, supplied the village of Pepe'ekeo with drinking water. It was only used as backup, in case of emergency. The county was drilling a backup well for the community, and then the spring and its infrastructure, which was another huge source of water, would revert to us. There was so much water that we eventually put in a 100 kilowatt hydroelectric system.

The different conditions at our two locations dictated how we operated and made our sustainability principles work. For instance, at Kea'au, we mainly farmed on rock. At Pepe'ekeo, there was plenty of soil, and grass grew wild between the bananas.

We soon realized that our tractors made ruts in the rows between plants if we kept using the same path, so we experimented with widening the distance between banana plants. That let us mow between rows, which meant our machines got traction on the grass and didn't make ruts. The grass trapped water and chemicals, too, so they didn't run off into the rivers.

We were always very adaptable, and some people called us innovators. We were always looking at change to make things better. I like change. It keeps things interesting and exciting.

Moving to Pepe'ekeo in 1994 turned out to be a great decision.

When we moved, we changed our company name to Hamakua Springs Country Farms.

We'd started in 1982 as Keaau Bananas, and then later took Mauna Kea Bananas as our corporate name. We sold our apple bananas under the Mauna Kea Bananas name.

After all those years, it was a big decision to change our company's name. We were emotionally invested in the Keaau Bananas name, and we wondered about the repercussions.

But it worked.

Our new name included "Hamakua," because that was the coast where the farm was located; "Springs," because our new land had three springs on it, and "Country Farms," because even though we now had 600 acres, we always thought of ourselves as small farmers. As we expanded the farms' products, I envisioned having a series of boutique-like farms rather than one big corporate identity.

We had the very talented Nelson Makua design our great, highly stylized Hamakua Springs Country Farms logo.

It was also in Pepe'ekeo that I started my Hamakua Springs blog "Ha Ha Ha" (the title referred to the farm being run by three generations of our Ha family). The writer Leslie Lang helped me start that blog and post to it two or three times a week most weeks from 2006 through 2017.

Leslie and I first met when the Hawaiian Airlines magazine Hana Hou assigned her to write an article about me. She interviewed me for about 20 minutes and then wrote an article that said exactly what I'd meant to say. I was so impressed and remember telling her that nobody had captured my message so accurately before. We've worked well together ever since.

What never changed after we moved to Pepeekeo was our commitment to sustainable farming. That was never just an ideal. It was everything.

Community members and visitors to the farm

In addition to supermarkets and restaurants, our bananas found their way to some interesting places.

For instance, one of the events we donated to every year was the Kilauea Volcano Run. More than one thousand people gather from around the world every summer to participate in the state's largest trail run, which takes place in the Hawai'i Volcanoes National Park, which is 4,000 feet up Kīlauea Volcano.

The run has an interesting history. It started modestly many years back when a Hawai'i Volcanoes National Park ranger wanted to "toughen up" his staff by having them run in the back country. And it truly is back country—runners climb crater walls and cross dirt trails, cooled lava fields, the sands of the Ka'ū Desert, and tropical rainforest.

Every year, we also donated bananas to my alma mater Hilo High's Grad Night, a fun, alcohol- and drug-free event for graduates. Often, 80 or 90 percent of the graduating seniors participate in Grad Night. The action starts immediately after the graduation ceremony and lasts until morning, usually at the Hilo Yacht Club.

Our bananas went into the make-your-own banana split activity. There was also pizza for dinner, all sorts of activities all night long, and then breakfast in the morning before the graduates were bused back to campus where their parents picked them up at 5 a.m. We liked being a small part of that celebration.

At one point, we wondered if offering farm tours would help us sell bananas, and among the groups we invited were schoolkids. My daughter Tracy took kindergartners and first-graders on tours of the farm and showed them how we grow bananas.

I remember one group she took around. They held hands and walked in small groups of two lines, each group with a teacher or adult volunteer in charge.

Tracy asked the kids if they knew which way bananas face when they are hanging on the tree. Up or down?

"UP!!" yelled some of the children enthusiastically. An equal number shouted, "DOWN!!" Some of them just yelled.

She showed them how workers cut the hands of bananas from stalks with a special air tool. And they got to see how the bananas are trimmed, washed, and then weighed and put in trays of forty pounds each.

After they learned how we carefully pack the bananas into boxes, being careful not to bruise them, the kids got a banana break. Each child got a banana, and they were the most enthusiastic bunch of banana eaters I've ever seen. I wondered if they were always that hungry. One kid ate three bananas.

We were flattered they liked our bananas so much. But I'm pretty sure any food would have been fine for those little bundles of energy.

Tracy told them that Kea'au Bananas, still our name at the time, were the best bananas of all.

At the end of the tour, hoping she'd gotten her message across, she asked: "Now kids, when your mommy goes to buy bananas at the market, which bananas will you tell her to buy?"

They replied, in unison: "YELLOW BANANAS!"

I laughed about that for a long time, and we stopped trying to market bananas to kindergartners. We continued to enjoy their visits, though.

One year, a gentleman from a large organic produce distributor in Tokyo visited the farm. We were exploring whether we might be able to export bananas to Japan.

The night before we showed him around the farm, we had dinner together. He was so formal and reserved that I felt a little uncomfortable about wearing shorts to dinner, as I always do.

The next day, we showed him our banana packing operation and explained our sustainable farming methods and food safety procedures. I couldn't tell what he was thinking.

We stood on the road alongside rows of bananas, and he saw how our harvester Albert Perreira notched the banana tree so it bent over just right. We watched as Albert put most of the banana bunch's weight on his shoulder. He cut the bunch off and didn't flinch as its weight, probably more than one hundred pounds, dropped onto his shoulder. He carried it to the trailer. It was a routine demonstration.

But then Albert went back to cut the tree down and move the pieces so they weren't in the way of the fertilizer tractor.

Our healthy banana trees had trunks as thick as a man's torso, and we used a razor-sharp machete with a two-foot blade to harvest them. Albert swung his machete once and it sliced completely through the tree about two feet off the ground. Before the trunk fell, and on the machete's backswing, he quickly chopped it into two more pieces.

Our quiet, reserved guest yelled, raised his arms, and leaped off the ground. I was so surprised! He'd been so staid, so serious, and hadn't smiled. It was the only reaction I saw from him.

But I instantly understood what he saw—a samurai warrior swinging his sword cleanly through an enemy.

That's what banana harvesters are like: samurai warriors.

Although that deal didn't end up happening, I always remembered his visit because he gave me such a completely different way of looking at harvesting bananas.

Three-wheelers and bananas

Not just anybody can become a banana harvester. It's the most physically demanding job on the farm by far. But it's not necessarily the biggest, strongest, or baddest person who is successful at harvesting. It's the person with the most determination and mental toughness.

I've seen lots of big, strong, and mean guys over the years who just could not handle the job. You have to be tough to be a banana harvester.

I'm proud to have been the original banana harvester more than twenty-five years ago. That's how I know what a difficult job it is, and it's why I always had such enormous respect for our banana harvesters. Good harvesters make it look easy, but it's not at all.

In Central and South America, workers carry the heavy banana bunches more than one hundred feet to a cable for transporting. But we came up with a system where our banana harvesters only needed to take a few steps with a bunch on their backs. We also designed our trailers so the harvesters didn't have to bend forward much to set down the bunch. And we used a winch system to lift the bunches off the trailer.

It wasn't because we were especially brilliant that we designed that system. Here's how it happened: I used to ride off-road dirt bikes for fun, and then the first three-wheelers came out. I had to have one of those toys, so I told June we could get one and use it on the farm for spraying. I explained that I could strap on the backpack sprayer, and then by riding on the three-wheeler, I could get more spraying done than when I walked.

Her reaction was, "Yeah, right." But we did get one. It was as fun as I thought it would be, and we did actually use it for spraying.

Then four-wheelers came out. They had lots of power and great suspension, so of course I had to have one of those, too.

"I know!" I told June. "We'll use one to pull the trailer when we harvest the bananas."

We designed the units so that harvesters only had to take about seven steps with a heavy banana bunch on their backs. The height was such that they didn't have to bend their backs much when they put the bunch onto the ATV-pulled trailer, and we ran the tires on five pounds of pressure, which prevented bouncing.

Win-win.

Our bananas weren't always picture-perfect on the outside. They looked real, like locally grown bananas, and that was a conscious decision. We, and other local growers, knew we could make them look prettier by using insecticide-impregnated bags, but we chose not to expose our workers—who had to carry those bags in close contact with their skin—to those chemicals.

And yet, it was ironic that our decision to protect our workers meant some stores wouldn't carry our bananas. They weren't blemish-free enough.

They still tasted good, though. People on O'ahu sometimes asked me where they could buy our bananas because they liked the taste. They weren't worried about small blemishes.

We were doing the right thing for our employees, and our decision didn't affect the taste of the bananas. "What's wrong with this picture?" I always asked myself.

Foodland was the only supermarket that supported our decision and carried our locally grown bananas. We always appreciated that. Otherwise, we could only sell them in Chinatown.

I once met someone who told me that bananas grow all over his home island of Madeira. He said they had some marks on them, but everybody liked them.

It was just the same with ours.

Our banana farm was doing great, and in 2002 we wanted to diversify. But first, we had to decide which new type of farming to go into.

There were signs that China's strong economic growth would require a tremendous amount of energy, so it was safe to assume that energy prices would rise. Again, focusing on principles of sustainability, we decided to go into a type of hydroponic production that took advantage of all the free sunlight and our abundant supply of water.

We planned to use the highest tech procedures possible in a low-tech structure. The idea was: why install air conditioning when you could just orient a growing house so that breezes pass through?

We always used sustainability as our primary guiding principle. Whenever we came to a fork in the road, we asked ourselves: "Which way will take us toward a sustainable future?" That gave us a reliable compass to follow.

Also in 2002, we were excited to learn that the farm was a finalist for the Patrick Madden Award for Sustainable

Agriculture. At that point, we had 800 acres of bananas growing on two farms.

The award, given by Sustainable Agriculture Research & Education (SARE), recognizes farmers or farm families that advance sustainable agriculture through innovation, leadership, and good stewardship. The award is named for SARE's first director, Patrick Madden, who was a pioneer in the movement toward strong, independent agriculture.

SARE's mission is to advance—to the whole of American agriculture—innovations that improve profitability, stewardship, and quality of life by investing in groundbreaking research and education.

Although we weren't ultimately chosen as the winner, we were very proud to be nominated. We were one of six U.S. farms recognized for what SARE described as our "long-term view, minimizing agri-chemicals, erosion, and water use, 'eco-friendly' labels, and crew of 70 workers enjoying profit-sharing."

Chapter 5

Becoming Uncle Tomato

I became known for tomatoes when we started growing them in a couple of experimental hydroponic greenhouses in about 2003.

If someone had told me back in high school, where the macho image was everything, that one day I'd be called The Banana Man, or Uncle Tomato, we would have had to go behind the gym and scrap!

We especially liked growing heirloom tomatoes, which are usually defined as varieties more than fifty years old. Heirlooms come from back when tomatoes were bred for their delicious taste, rather than for how nice they look and how far they can be shipped.

When your primary goals are to grow disease-resistant tomatoes that are attractive and have a long shelf life, heirlooms are not your first choice.

But we grew them, and chefs loved them because they taste delicious, both raw and cooked.

One variety we grew is called Striped German. They are pretty, two-toned tomatoes that are bright yellow with a starburst of red. When you slice them, you see pinks and yellows. They are sweet with just a hint of acid. People who like sweet tomatoes love them.

We also grew a dark, almost black variety called Purple Cherokee. Those are more meaty, or "beefy." They have a consistent texture throughout and the seeds don't tend to fall out. I like Purple Cherokees chilled and sliced with a little Hawaiian salt and ground black pepper. They, too, have a nice balance of sweetness to acid.

We sold our popular heirlooms in one-pound clamshell containers at local supermarkets.

Back when Hilo Bay Café was still, incongruously, located in the strip mall next to Walmart, Chef Josh had a sampler platter of our heirloom tomatoes on the menu. It was a simple but striking presentation—a platter with thick wedges of different types and colors of heirlooms, a small mound of deep red 'alae salt from Kaua'i for dipping, and a mound of cracked black pepper.

I thought it was great that Chef Josh had enough confidence in his ability just to let the tomatoes do what they do—sit there and shine. What an artist.

When we heard about the Tomato Fest in Carmel, California, which was dedicated to the heirloom tomato, June and I had to go.

We found a huge tent entirely dedicated to displaying and providing samples of heirloom tomatoes, every kind you could possibly imagine. It was like being inside a Dr. Seuss book. There were big ones, little ones, red ones, green ones, purple ones, white ones, yellow ones with stripes, round ones, long ones and everything in between—more than two hundred varieties set out in a long line where people could sample them.

There were also chefs making amazing dishes with the heirlooms. One was a tomato tower made of caramelized onions and slices of different-colored cocktail-sized heirloom tomatoes. We tasted a sorbet made with tomatoes, sauteed leeks, something sweet, and a hint of basil.

We really liked a tomato shooter consisting of yellow, Lemon Boy tomato soup with a red heirloom tomato soup layered on top. The instructions read: "Sip the red soup and notice the burn, and then drink the rest of the Lemon Boy soup with syrup to top it off."

It was so interesting and fun to see what people were doing with heirloom tomatoes.

Red-Ribbon tomatoes

Our primary tomato product was the tasty, well-liked Hamakua Springs cocktail tomato.

Lynne Rossetto Kasper, who hosts American Public Media's radio program "The Splendid Table"—its target audience is "people who love to eat"—came to Kapi'olani Community College one year and taught a three-hour master class on tomatoes. She called it "Tomato 101."

As part of her master class, she and one hundred professional chefs and culinary students held a tomato-tasting. And we won! Our Hamakua Springs cocktail tomatoes were judged the best-tasting tomatoes, and it was during the winter, too. It was a big deal because all the growers entered their best products and there were a lot of high-level chefs in the class.

Also, the television program Top Chef taped here on the Big Island once. When finalist Marcel Vigneron was selecting ingredients for the final competition, he tasted one of our Hamakua Springs tomatoes and immediately loaded up his basket. One of the show's chef consultants took some of our tomatoes with her to eat. Offhandedly, she mentioned that where she lives, there are no good tomatoes in the winter.

We also grew small, crunchy, green tomatoes called Green Zebras and tiny, tear-shaped Hamakua Sweets, which were so sweet they almost tasted like you'd sprinkled sugar on them. Those were our favorites, and they were always a big hit with customers, too.

We started growing the Hamakua Sweets after, at the heirloom tomato festival, we saw a little girl, maybe eight years old, grab some of that variety, eat them, take some more, eat them, and then go back for more! I figured she was young and her test buds were probably better than mine.

One reason our tomatoes were so tasty was that we deliberately selected varieties for taste rather than any other quality. And we didn't harvest until the fruit was ripe on the vine, meaning we let them develop complex flavors.

Because our operation was hydroponic—soil-free—we didn't have any soil-borne insects, and we used weed cloth so we didn't have to spray.

Nutritional value of our tomatoes

Early on, I read that U.S. Department of Agriculture data showed the nutritional value of fruits and vegetables had declined over the past 50 years. In some cases, they were dramatic changes, ranging from a 6 percent decrease in protein to 38 percent less riboflavin.

I thought about how we didn't normally focus on nutrient levels in the vegetables we grew, and decided we would do something about it to the extent we could. I definitely wanted to tilt in that direction. If we could get great-tasting, happy plants and vegetables that were more nutrient-dense than the ones we'd grown six months before, we'd be really happy.

Charlotte Romo was our hydroponic crop specialist then. She agreed with the scientist quoted in the article who said the nutrient decrease was likely due to changed agricultural practices.

Charlotte told me that farmers started using synthesized chemicals in the fields after World War II and based everything on what the plant needed. They tried to pump up the plant to grow fast and yield a lot of fruit, but that didn't necessarily produce quality fruit in terms of nutrition.

Fifty years ago, she added, there were lots of little farms located everywhere. But now, there are primarily giant farms that do what's good for shipping and not necessarily what's best for food quality.

I'd never heard of fertilizing and growing plants for their nutrient component. Increasing nutrients isn't something most people talk about. But it just seemed right to me that vegetables should have as many nutrients as possible, so we decided to try. Common sense.

So we made a plan. First, we determined our current nutrient levels. Charlotte sent tomatoes off to the lab on O'ahu for nutritional analyses on the fruit itself, whereas previously, we'd only checked leaves. Leaf analysis was common, she said. It tells you what the plant needs, but it doesn't tell you anything about nutrients in the part of the plant we eat.

We were happy when we got the lab results back and saw they showed a good nutrition profile. We kept using the fertilizer formula that had raised the nutrition level. We weren't doing it as a selling point. We weren't going to advertise and say ours were better than the next. We just knew it was the right thing to do.

It's the same as when we decided to become ECO-OK for producing our bananas in an environmentally responsible manner. And when we decided to become Food Safety Certified.

It was just the right thing to do. Our focus is always on what's the right thing to do.

Our tomato correspondents

People actually used to write to us about our tomatoes. We got a lot of amazing, unsolicited letters like these three:

> Aloha! My husband and I are visiting here from Tennessee. Tennessee prides itself on its great produce, and with good reason. Nevertheless, I have experienced your cocktail tomatoes, and they are unequaled! What a taste! Sooooo good! Y'all come see us some time!

> Dear Hamakua Springs,

> I just bought some of your grape tomatoes from Times, and they are the best-tasting tomatoes I've had in 23 years on Oahu! Firm, sweet and delicious. Thank you so much! I have been trying to grow my own but with little success. Yours will definitely fill my "tomato gap." Thanks again for a great product, and keep up the good work. P.S. My family and I appreciate the de-emphasis on pesticide use.

> Your Cocktail Tomatoes, and regular size Tomatoes, are the very best we have ever tasted! And we have tasted many different ones.

A couple years in a row, we held a community-wide tomato recipe contest that we called the "You Say Tomato" contest. Just as there are different ways to pronounce the word, we explained, people cook with tomatoes differently, too.

The three categories were entrée, salad, and preserves/condiments.

First, judges narrowed down the recipes that came in, and then thirty students from the Hawai'i Community College food service program did a great job preparing the top five recipes in each category. Their instructions were to prepare the recipes exactly, without improvising.

Our judges were Randy Nunokawa, Audrey Wilson, Rockne Freitas, Marlene Hapai, Joan Namkoong, and Sonia Martinez, who did an amazing job organizing it all. When the judging was over, all the dishes went onto a buffet line, and everybody made a plate and sampled the tomato dishes. They were absolutely delicious.

Sharing the tomato wealth

Sometimes we had unexpected spikes in tomato production. Since we only harvested when our tomatoes were vine-ripe, we couldn't hold onto them long when there were extras. We had to move them quickly.

We asked ourselves what we should do when that occurred and realized we wanted to support our community. Our sustainable farming philosophy meant we were always concerned about our workers, our community, and the environment. But how?

One time, we decided to give the extras to our county workers. They aren't recognized enough and we wanted to acknowledge their hard work. So I called over to the county building and said I had some extra cocktail tomatoes.

Dayday Hopkins, Economic Development Specialist at the Hawai'i County Department of Research and Development, asked me how many tomatoes I was talking about. I told her twenty-five cases, and she was so surprised. She said she thought I meant a case or two.

She got some help, and we went around to all the offices in the county building: planning, parks and recreation, civil service, finance, office of the aging, corporation council, and others. I also took some cases to the department of water supply, which isn't located in that building.

Dayday even sent some to the mayor's office, where they were a hit. Mayor Harry Kim called her and asked if there was any way he could get two more containers. (He got them.)

She told me some of the workers were surprised and even suspicious when we handed them containers of tomatoes. They thought we were trying to sell them. She said people also mentioned being surprised they were such beautiful, perfect tomatoes and not "seconds," or tomatoes that weren't nice enough to sell.

Another time we gave extra tomatoes to public safety personnel. We had enough cocktail tomatoes to give one container to every firefighter and EMT on the Big Island. They told us they were really grateful that someone from the community felt moved to do such a thing.

I told them our workers are happy to work for a company that can do it. We appreciate all that fire personnel do for our community. It's a win-win situation for everybody.

Heading out to the schools

Sometimes when we had those inevitable spikes in tomato production, we found an elementary school with the same number of teachers as we had containers of extra tomatoes, and took our extras to the school. But we didn't want to leave anyone out, so we decided only to choose schools where we had enough to give to everybody on the staff.

Once, we had ninety-seven boxes of Hamakua Springs cocktail tomatoes to give out. That was 776 individual "clamshell" containers. We gave one clamshell to every staff member at the following schools: Kalaniana'ole Elementary, Waiākea Elementary, Waiākeawaena Elementary, Kea'au Elementary,

Kea'au Middle, Mountain View Elementary, Pāhoa Elementary, and Kaumana Elementary.

We put a note in each container saying how much we appreciate the work they do for our keiki. We felt so good about being able to recognize these important members of our community. I am especially partial toward elementary school teachers. The most impressionable time of my life was when I was between eight and eleven years old. That was when my belief system formed, and it lasted all my life.

Eventually, we made our way down the coast to all the elementary schools: Hilo Union, Chiefess Kapi'olani, Waiākea, Kalani'ana'ole, and Ha'aheo. Finally, we ended up at Keonepoko in Hawaiian Beaches.

Sometimes we gave to the students, too. We decided on elementary schools because our tomatoes were something young kids could take home to their parents. I felt pretty good being able to do that.

Over the years, I've been floored by all the people I don't know who come up and tell me they were so happy to receive tomatoes. Some of the most touching and rewarding moments have been when teachers I've never met came up and thanked us for giving them Hamakua Springs tomatoes.

It was especially meaningful, I think, at a time when newspapers were reporting that this or that school was in danger of restructuring under the No Child Left Behind federal program. We knew teachers were having a rough time and that morale was at a low point. That was precisely why we wanted to make clear that we thought they were the greatest! We feel strongly that teaching is the most important profession. And we wanted to tell each teacher that we supported them 100 percent.

Another reason we support our teachers is that education really is the great equalizer. Hawai'i Community College (HCC) Chancellor Rockne Freitas explains it best: He says that the best predictor of children's success is the family's household income. And the best predictor of a higher household income is education. Hawai'i Community College is one of the most important institutions of higher learning here in East Hawai'i because it has open enrollment. In other words, there isn't an entrance exam to keep students out. Also, HCC class credits are transferrable to the University of Hawai'i at Hilo.

On the east side of the Big Island, we have disproportionately more than the state's average of low-income families. Hawai'i Community College is a pathway to higher education for students who might not otherwise qualify.

HCC ranked thirteenth in the nation at bringing higher education to its students. This despite having the most dilapidated classrooms and structures in the entire community college system. It's a huge deal, and Chancellor Freitas and his staff deserve a big round of applause. These people are doers, not talkers. We respect that!

Kids write the darnedest things

One day in 2004, after we took surplus tomatoes to Hilo Union School, Emma Kato's 4th-grade class sent us wonderful thank you letters. Ms. Kato wrote: "We always ask our students to reach out to others to make lives better. You certainly did that to us."

The most interesting part of giving tomatoes to students was always reading the notes they sent afterward. I read every one. They were really impressive and fun to read. Here are a few:

> Dear Mr. Ha,
>
> Thank you for the tomatoes. It was de-licious. It was juicey and sweet. It was like healthy candy in my mouth. I just ate the tomatoes for lunch, plain like a fruit.
>
> Aloha, Alohi

Dear Mr. Ha.

Thanks for the fantastic tomato's. When we went on the computer I learned that the benefets of growing with hydroponics are they avoid pests and deaseses. And the energy costs are lower. And I also learned that your farm grows award-winning tomatos, bananas, lettuce and cucumbers that are available throughout Hawaii.

When I brought the tomatos home, my grandpa from Phillipines made some kind of tomato sauce that taste good with rice and fish.

Aloha, Patrick

Dear Mr. Ha,

Thanks for giving us the tomatoes, it was good. I ate my tomatoes and gave some to my parents. Thank you for thinking about Hilo Union and giving us the tomatoes to eat. That was a nice thing to do. So good luck and plant some more tomatoes.

Joseph

When we had a short, sharp spike in tomato production in 2007, we gave some of our extras to Keonepoko Elementary School students, teachers, and staff. We were looking to give out several hundred one-pound containers of cocktail tomatoes and chose Keonepoko because it's a large school.

Here are some of the letters they later sent:

Dear Mr. Richard Ha,

Thank you for the tomatose. The tomatoes is very good. My family love the tomatse. Some time we play tomato fight. Then we plant the seed to grow more tomato.

Sincerely, Kaysen

Dear Mr. Richard Ha,

Thank you Mr Richard. I liked the tomatoes. I really liked it. I throw a tomato at my fraind. Do you plant the tomatoes? My dad used to plant them when he was working with plants.

Sincerely, Savannah

Hi Mr. Richard Ha and Hamakua Springs, I thank you for the delicious tomatos and thank you for donateing.

Sincerely, Jensen

P.S. Please come again.

Chapter 6

Chefs Who Make a Difference

One year when we were doing our Adopt-a-Class program, Chef Alan Wong adopted Keaukaha Elementary School's whole sixth grade. Adopt-a-Class was a program where community members could donate money so a specific class at a particular school could take field trips that the school couldn't otherwise afford.

Chef Alan asked if he could speak to the sixth-graders he adopted. So he flew in from Honolulu one day and we drove over to Keaukaha to meet them.

A PBS crew was preparing a Chefs Afield television episode about Alan Wong at the time and they filmed the whole morning, which started with the students chanting a Hawaiian welcome.

Chef Alan is great with kids. He's a natural-born teacher, and the Keaukaha students really responded to him. They were very engaged as he showed them how to make homemade mayonnaise and a li hing mui salad dressing.

He told them that when he was growing up he thought salad dressing only came out of a bottle. Look how far he's come, he was saying. He said, "If Alan Wong can do it, you can do it. You just have to work hard." They, too, can achieve anything, he told them.

As he cooked, he pointed out how reading was essential to what he was doing, and which parts used math, and in what ways it had to do with science. He made the point that if they wanted to do that kind of job, they needed to stay in school.

He had started his talk by asking how many kids hated tomatoes, and most raised their hands. But in the end, when he did a taste test, they were believers. He let them compare pieces of a "Brand X" tomato and a Hamakua Springs one, and they loved it. When some of his people walked around with platters of cut-up heirloom tomatoes, kids were actually lunging for them, trying to get more. It was something else.

I spoke, too, and told the students that when I was their age, we were poor. We had a picnic table in the kitchen for our dinner table, I said, and my father used to pound that table and say, "Not 'no can.' 'CAN!'"

I told those kids, "Can!" I told them they could do anything they wanted with their lives.

Afterward, some of the students showed Chef Alan and me their kalo (taro) patch. I chatted with the school's principal, Kumu Lehua Veincent, and he told me they never get people of such celebrity speaking to, and inspiring, their kids.

With tears in her eyes, one of the teachers told me that no one ever goes to Keaukaha Elementary to tell the students they can do it. I was very glad Chef Alan offered to speak to those kids.

Honored at a Farmers Series dinner

Sometime after that, Chef Alan invited us to one of his Farmers Series dinners. At each dinner, he featured a particular grower whose products he serves. It was the first dinner of the current series, and he was featuring Hamakua Springs. What an honor.

Several of us flew over to Honolulu. It was me, June, our daughter Tracy, her husband Kimo, who was the farm's manager, and their daughter Kimberly.

Before the dinner, Chef Alan asked us to speak to his staff. I introduced each of us and talked about where we came from, what we all do on the farm, and why it's important to us. I talked about how what they do supports our efforts. I spoke about energy and geothermal and how they are related to food security.

It felt great to help his staff gain a better understanding of who we are and what we do. They were very knowledgeable and attentive, and I learned they really do know who grows their produce. We talked for about an hour before the dinner began.

When people arrived and were seated, the staff took us around to each table and introduced us. We told the diners what we do, and every person said they support local agriculture. Every single one. It was striking.

Some customers asked if we went around and worked with other chefs and restaurants, too. We told them no, that Alan Wong was the only chef that does that.

His efforts in making sure his farmers and restaurant staff know and respect each other helped us farmers feel even more responsible for our products. Chef Alan depended on us to provide the freshest produce for them, and not only our family but everybody working at the farm understood that. So instead of leaving our products at the loading dock and never thinking about them again, we realized we were responsible for them until they are on the plate in front of the customer.

Chef Alan demonstrated the difference between fresh-grown Hamakua Springs tomatoes and tomatoes from a can. For the first course, he made two soups—one from Hamakua Springs tomatoes and the other from tomatoes from a can.

I got a huge kick out of what he called that tasting: "Not No Can...Can! Tomatoes."

Then he conducted a taste test. Hands down, diners preferred the Hamakua Springs tomato soup.

He also made two versions of stewed tomatoes, one from canned tomatoes and one with our fresh tomatoes, and served them in saimin spoons. The one he made with canned tomatoes was dark red and had an aftertaste. The one with our tomatoes was lighter. You could taste a huge difference, and everybody commented on it.

June's favorite course was the lobster ravioli. It was a two-inch ravioli stuffed with lobster pieces with a buttery corn sauce on top.

It's very unusual for a chef to make farmers and others feel important the way Alan does. It was great to have Kimo, Tracy, and Kimberly there with us. They were the next generation and it felt important that they experience the same feelings we did. That's really valuable.

Pulling for the farmers

Another chef and restaurateur who made a big difference was Peter Merriman. Many years ago, chefs like Alan Wong and Peter Merriman couldn't get fresh produce locally. They had to import it from the U.S. mainland.

The chefs made it known that they would pay well for fresh produce grown locally. They encouraged local farmers to start growing specifically for them and just bring their produce to the back door and get paid directly. That was pretty revolutionary at the time, and it was the start of what became known as Hawai'i Regional Cuisine.

So what was being grown locally started being diverted to the chefs. Farmers started making more money and could afford to grow their businesses. What was happening gave farmers hope that they could produce a good quality product and be sustainable.

At that time, I heard that Peter Merriman, who was working at one of the Kohala Coast resorts, said, "I'd like to see one of my farmers drive up in a Mercedes Benz."

What was happening over there didn't affect me at the time. I was growing bananas in Hilo, on the other side of the island. Peter probably had no idea who I was.

But I was so impressed by his statement and what it represented that I called Peter at home and thanked him on behalf of farmers everywhere. We both remember that day many years ago.

Part 2

The Problems

It was about 2004 when I noticed our costs at the farm were starting to increase. It wasn't only our costs that were going up, though. I knew that, at the same time, our customers' discretionary incomes were also increasingly getting "squeezed."

It was clearly related to oil costs, and I started thinking about a future where oil supplies continued to decline. I knew our input costs would continue to rise as a consequence, and that people would have less discretionary income. Higher prices and having less money to spend on needs are a bad combination.

Fast forward to 2006. Growth in China and other factors were pushing energy costs even higher than we expected. Gasoline cost more than $3 per gallon.

I was so glad we'd decided to move the farm to Pepe'ekeo. And boy was I glad we hadn't gone into a high-energy system of production. On the contrary, our Hamakua Springs brand had become known for its hydroponic vegetables.

In 2008, the price of oil hit $147 per barrel and I thought the world had changed forever. Business as usual was no longer possible.

How would we adapt? How could we change and still produce enough food to feed Hawai'i's people?

I kept asking myself how we could use small farmer skills and resources on our larger farm so the whole would be more than just the sum of its parts. We needed to make our farm relevant for the future. And could we make it fun, too, as well as productive?

We had no idea just how high oil prices would rise, nor that there was a global pandemic in our future.

Chapter 7

Costs Through the Roof

In early 2008, the most interesting thing happened at the farm. I could never have imagined it. It was like something out of a movie.

First, let me set the scene. Since the year before, I'd been feeling a bit like a frog in a pot on the stove. As the temperature increases a little bit at a time, the frog doesn't notice the water getting hotter—until he is, well, done.

"Hmm, it's getting warmer. Kinda cozy. But, wait. How come bubbles are starting to rise? I'm getting outta here!"

Fertilizer, chemicals, packaging, and transportation were all more expensive than ever before. We don't always realize how much petroleum products are involved in almost every facet of our lives, and when the cost of goods starts going up, it's easy to miss that it's due to a rise in petroleum prices.

It's like that frog, sitting in a pot on the stove, who doesn't realize that the temperature is slowly increasing.

The news said that inflation was under control, everything was all right, and the stock market was at near record levels.

But if everything was all right, how come fertilizer cost so much more? And how come the plastic clamshells and plastic bags we used cost so much now? How come all our various types of supplies were so much more expensive?

We started noticing the phrase "fuel adjustment fee" showing up on bills. I knew agricultural costs were steadily rising, but what really raised alarm bells was when I complained about the rise in oil prices to a lawyer friend.

He replied, "Oh yeah, the mom-and-pop plate lunch places are suffering, too, because plastic containers and utensils are more expensive now and they can't easily pass the cost on."

I realized that rising oil prices were affecting people in all sorts of businesses. So I started reading a lot of articles about oil supply and demand and that was my wake-up call.

If I were a frog, I would have jumped out of the pot, hit the floor, and ran straight for the exit.

In March 2008, Aloha Airlines—which we'd flown back and forth between the Hawaiian Islands since 1946—filed for bankruptcy protection and stopped its passenger service. Our distributor told us some farmers were having to dip into their savings to buy fertilizer. We started noticing fewer abandoned cars on roadsides, and I learned that scrap metal prices made it worth hauling abandoned vehicles away.

Weyerhaeuser, the corrugated box manufacturing company on Oʻahu, closed. More than half of all Hawaiʻi's agricultural products, including years' worth of ours, were packed in Weyerhaeuser boxes. HMSA, which provides health insurance to more than half of Hawaiʻi's population, announced a substantial rate hike. Steel prices were going up, so the cost of maintaining the farm's growing houses increased.

To me, the most worrisome part was that farmers cannot control their prices. Farmers are price-takers, not price-makers. In other words, they have to take the price that wholesalers or retailers will give them, no matter what their costs are.

We knew what was happening. We live in a finite world and resources are limited. Do we just sit in the pot and watch ourselves cook?

At the same time that fertilizer, energy, and healthcare costs for our employees were soaring, banana prices were flat. I was watching our costs and profits closely, and just about every week I saw our profits gradually, but steadily, drop.

Our main problem was that we couldn't get enough workers to keep the essential jobs on schedule. That, coupled with rising fertilizer and other costs, was resulting in low yields and poor production.

We tried to shut down the bananas—but failed

In April, I talked seriously with Kimo Pa, my son-in-law and farm manager. I spoke with June and with Tracy. We all agreed it wasn't looking good. It wasn't sustainable.

I thought it would be better to shut down the business sooner, while we were still doing all right, rather than being forced to do so later.

So on a Friday in early April, I had a tough talk with my workers. I told them I was going to have to shut down the banana operation and I explained why. I told them we would meet again Monday to talk about who was interested in taking a different job on the farm.

It was on Monday that the most unexpected thing happened.

Seven of our nine workers came back to work with a plan for how to keep the banana business going. They huddled with Kimo for hours and, together, they sketched out a plan for how we could be more efficient and profitable, and keep going.

I was stunned.

Their idea was to remove the 100 acres of apple bananas, which are more labor-intensive and yield less profit. Then we would move the remaining bananas much closer to our packing house and refrigeration units, reduce the workload, and speed up turnaround. That way, they said, we could operate with a smaller workforce and get a higher output, which would be enough to make a healthy profit.

They really wanted this plan to succeed and assured us they would put in the labor to make it happen.

It could work, I realized. The ever-increasing price of oil was starting to work to our farm's advantage in one way—imports were having to pay a 30 percent or higher fuel surcharge to ship to Hawai'i. And I knew that our electric bill, which was $15,000 per month because of our coolers, would soon go down because I was installing a hydroelectric generator.

Kimo and I talked, saw that higher prices for imported bananas might help us, and decided to give the workers' plan a try.

The next day, I gathered the workers and agreed to their new, streamlined plan. They smiled and got to work.

They pulled out apple banana trees and prepared that land so we could lease it to other farmers. Closer to our packing and cooling operation, they planted Williams bananas.

I cannot describe how impressed I was with our employees and their commitment to making it work.

And so we kept going.

I wanted to lease the former apple banana land to farmers who lived in or very near Pepe'ekeo so they could walk or travel a very short distance to work. That would keep their travel costs minimal as energy costs continued to rise. Farmers who joined us could also choose to have us market their product if they wanted.

We talked with farmers and listened to their plans to see if they fit into our program. They needed to fit into our criteria of sustainability.

The more different things we, and they, grew, the better we could serve our community. We were already producing hydroponic vegetables—tomatoes, lettuce, cucumbers, green onions, and others—which we sold to Hawai'i supermarkets and restaurants under our Hamakua Springs Country Farms brand. We expanded our hydroponics operation by adding twenty new planting houses for tomatoes and other produce.

What was driving our changes was the need to adapt to our changing environment. It all came down to rising oil prices. I was always trying to see where we needed to be five and ten years down the road. People who don't adapt to changing conditions are invariably replaced by others who do.

If we hadn't changed, we would have been history.

So we continued with bananas. A handful of years later, we heard from Yogurtland's "flavorologist" Scott Shoemaker, who tasted our bananas at the Farmers Market. He was impressed with their taste, and asked if he could come by the farm and hear our story.

As I showed him around the farm, I told him we are located right where prevailing tradewinds meet the slopes of Mauna Kea and drop plenty of rain, which we measure in feet instead of inches (11 feet per year!). Bananas love all that water. Also, our soil comes from volcanic cinder. The combination of excellent drainage and water retention is unusual and very good for banana production.

Not only did Yogurtland declare our bananas "Best in the World," but it also selected them to use in their Bananas Foster frozen yogurt. What an honor.

One day our friend Tisha Uehara, vice president of Armstrong Produce, called and asked if she could bring Chef Morimoto for a visit. He's a highly acclaimed chef with restaurants in several countries who is well-known for his appearances on the TV show Iron Chef.

She said he was opening a restaurant in Waikiki soon and wanted to introduce himself to Hawai'i farmers. Of course, we told her we would love to see him.

They swooped in like a whirlwind. Chef Morimoto really zeroed in on our grape and beef tomatoes. He looked at them closely and then just bit into one. Then he took several more bites and said he wanted them in his restaurant. He said the flavor was excellent and pointed out the thickness of the skin was just right.

He autographed some items, gave me an signed copy of his cookbook, and they were gone. It was a quick visit but we all really enjoyed it.

It was a thrill to read that Barack and Michelle Obama usually eat at Morimoto's Waikiki when they visit his hometown. The Obamas have probably enjoyed our tomatoes. Tomatoes fit for a president!

Chapter 8

Farmers Aren't Criminals

In all my years of farming, I never saw farmers so concerned about one issue, nor as united as they were around what happened in 2013.

What happened was that, although every major scientific organization in the world has endorsed the use of genetically modified organisms (GMOs), two anti-GMO bills popped up on the Big Island.

The first would have banned GMOs completely. If it passed, all GMO crops would have had to be removed within 30 months. Anyone failing to comply would have been fined $1,000 or sent to jail for 30 days. It would have made criminals out of farmers.

It was unfathomable. In Hawai'i's history, farmers were always revered, not criminalized.

I never grew any GMO crops, nor had any financial or other affiliation with any of the large seed or other companies that advocate for the use of GMOs. But I have always felt so strongly that we need to follow the science. We need to be sure we'll be able to feed all our people on this island in the future.

Sometimes, we may need to protect our farms from disease by using crops that are genetically modified.

Fortunately, after four days of debate and with sentiments running high, the Hawai'i County Council withdrew the bill.

But then the councilwoman who had proposed the first anti-GMO bill returned with a second, similar bill.

That one exempted two crops: corn, which an island dairy was growing to feed its cows, and papayas. Papaya farmers would have been required to register with the County and pay an annual $100 fee to be exempt.

Other than those two exceptions, no new, open-air cultivation of GMO crops would be allowed. Violators would be fined $1,000 per day and responsible for any legal, court, and other costs.

Farmers were horrified. For one thing, they pointed out that this ban would only affect Hawai'i Island farmers. Growers on other islands would still be able to use biotech solutions for any future insect and disease problems that cropped up, and therefore would have a strong advantage. Big Island farmers wouldn't be able to compete.

It was a huge and valid concern. What if, for instance, someone develops a plant that emits a pheromone that repels insects? That would save cost and labor—but both our conventional and organic farmers would be unable to grow this plant. They would be at a severe disadvantage compared to farmers on other islands.

Another example is the sweet potato, which grows very well on the Hamakua Coast. What if, one day, scientists transfer a gene from the sweet potato to the russet potato, making the russet resistant to fungus? That would eliminate the need for farmers to use fifteen applications of pesticide spray per season—but it wouldn't be allowed on Hawai'i Island.

Papaya farmers did not want anything to do with the new bill's exemption, saying it would unfairly stigmatize papayas. They worried that registering their papaya fields might also lead to activists targeting them.

The Rainbow papaya is an engineered, or GMO, variety that includes a gene that academic researchers developed. The gene makes the plant resistant to the ringspot virus. Scientists, independent experts, and farmers all agree that without it, ringspot virus would have destroyed the island's entire papaya industry.

Rainbow papayas account for three-quarters of the thirty million pounds of papaya harvested on Hawai'i Island every year. They are "cleaner" papayas, meaning they require fewer pesticides because farmers don't need to spray for the insects that cause ringspot virus.

Hawai'i-born scientist Dennis Gonsalves led the team that developed the Rainbow papaya. In 2002, they received the Humboldt Prize for the "most significant contribution to U.S. agriculture in five years."

Hawai'i Island farmers, who aim to be good stewards of the land, were distressed that this bill could force them to use more pesticides than farmers in the rest of the state.

They asked how it was possible that farmers who grow GMO crops would become criminals. For growing the food we eat?

I attended county council meetings to give testimony against that second bill, and it was an incredible scene. The testimony was inconsiderate and even mean at times.

The county council Skyped in an "expert" from the mainland named Jeffrey Smith, despite him having no scientific credentials.

I was incredulous when I read what Michael Specter wrote in *The New Yorker*: that although *The Dr. Oz Show* had presented

Smith as a "scientist," Smith actually had zero scientific experience or relevant qualifications.

The New Yorker also quoted Bruce Chassy, a molecular biologist and food scientist, who wrote to *The Dr. Oz Show* saying that Smith's "only professional experience prior to taking up his crusade against biotechnology is as a ballroom-dance teacher, yogic flying instructor, and political candidate for the Maharishi cult's natural-law party."

Discover magazine wrote that Smith would figure prominently in a section about pseudoscience: "He is the equivalent of an anti-vaccine leader, someone who is quite successful in spreading fear and false information."

Still, the county council chose Smith as its expert against GMOs. They gave him 45 minutes to speak. It was unbelievable.

They declined to call on any of the several University of Hawai'i scientists who'd flown in from O'ahu.

They did not consult any farmers.

Anyone wanting to speak who had a scientific background and expertise on the subject was discounted as having been "paid by biotech companies." It was very irresponsibly one-sided, in my opinion.

The New York Times sent its reporter Amy Harmon to cover the whole ugly situation. She wrote an excellent article titled, "A Lonely Quest for Facts on Genetically Modified Crops," (dated January 4, 2014, it's available online and worth a read) about Council Member Greggor Ilagan's careful research into GMOs.

The anti-GMO bill passed.

But we farmers filed a lawsuit in U.S. District Court and got the law overturned. Plaintiffs included Hawaii Papaya Industry Association president Ross Sibucao, cattle rancher Jason Moniz, floral growers Gordon Inouye and Eric Tanouye,

Pacific Floral Exchange, Biotechnology Industry Organization, and myself.

Some people worry that big mainland seed companies will come to the Big Island and set up shop. But that's not going to happen. They would just lose money, which is why they're not already here. They need flat land, low humidity, high sunlight, deep soil, and irrigation. Big tractors make money on the straightaways and lose money on the turns. Because the Big Island is so young geologically, we don't have the conditions to support industrial-scale agriculture.

It's counterintuitive, but in spite of its size, the Big Island is an environment that is best suited for small farmers, not large ones. We cannot let an irrational fear of industrialization cause us to make decisions that kill off our small farmers.

What's still clear to me, now more than ever, is that we need to keep looking forward. Hawai'i is isolated, and one of the least food-secure places in the world. We need to leverage our resources to find a competitive advantage and make sure we can continue to feed our people and produce quality food they can afford.

Organic farming cannot provide sufficient and affordable food for the masses here in Hawai'i, and is not the answer. We don't have enough manure for compost to provide nitrogen for fertilizer. Nitrogen, an essential nutrient for plants, is easily lost from the soil system and is often the most limiting nutrient in crop productivity.

We also don't have winter conditions that kill off bugs and provide an automatic reset.

We can leverage sun energy, which is both a plus and a minus. It's a plus because we have almost constant sun. It can be a minus because it causes weeds, insects, and diseases to thrive.

If we could grow crops that repel insects, that would mean we would need and use fewer pesticides. What if we could develop crops that generate their own nitrogen from the air? What if we had peaches, pears, apples, and cherries that thrive in our climate? This sort of research is already taking place right here on the Big Island.

Less need for pesticides and fertilizers, more food, and more discretionary income would benefit all Big Island farmers. And it would mean lower food costs for the "rubbah slippah" folk. That's what I call the ordinary people—the people who walk around in rubbah slippahs instead of shiny shoes. (Note: I am one of the rubbah slippah folk.)

Another benefit of the rubbah slippah people having more discretionary income is that they would spend more money locally, and businesses would thrive.

This would result in a better life for everybody.

Chapter 9

End of Our Tomatoes

In 2014, we made another very difficult decision and began phasing out our tomato production.

It happened because of something I'd been talking about for years. The skyrocketing price of oil had raised farming costs substantially. The pluses of growing our hydroponic tomatoes no longer exceeded the minuses.

Back in 2002 when we started growing tomatoes, we were banana growers. Oil prices were low and so were banana prices. It was hard to make a living that way and we needed to diversify.

That's one of the reasons we went into tomatoes. At the time, it was a good decision.

But over the years, our costs started increasing drastically. After a while, we knew our tomato-growing infrastructure was going to need to be replaced. We had to do some serious thinking. Should we take our tomato houses apart and rebuild them? Or replace them altogether?

Replacing them, it turned out, would cost three times what it had cost when we put them up twelve years earlier. That was eye-opening.

It was a real-world consequence of the price of oil going up so much. At that point, oil cost four times more than it had just ten years before, and that had significant consequences. Everything cost so much more. We were in the middle of major changes—still are—and most people don't even realize it.

As we were making that big decision about our tomatoes, we took into account that our customers were also under increasing economic pressure. They had less disposable income, also due to the effects of the rising cost of oil, and our tomatoes were a high-end product.

Another thing we knew, as we considered what to do about our tomato houses, was that we could expect oil and other costs to keep going up.

Our plan had always been to take our tomato farming to the next step. We were putting in a hydroelectric plant and wanted to use hydropower to grow our tomatoes in a controlled environment that excluded insects and optimized light and temperature. Unfortunately, though, it just took too long to get our hydropower plant operating.

We thought about it carefully for quite some time. Not only did we take all that into account, but also our next generation and what was best for them.

As difficult as it was to make the decision to stop growing tomatoes, we all agreed it was the right thing to do. It allowed us to continue farming as we weren't closing up shop but just going out of tomatoes.

We refocused our farming efforts based on the economic factors around us.

We stayed in bananas, which do well in our rain, deep soil, and other conditions. We knew the banana infrastructure we had in place, such as coolers and concrete, was good for another twenty years. In that situation, the pluses exceeded the minuses.

I was also interested in producing a cost-effective source of protein right there on the farm, such as tilapia and other fish. We were working on the problems of protein feed and oxygenation of water, which we could do with gravity and electricity. In this, as in all decisions, we were thinking about where we needed to be in ten or twenty years.

When we announced we would no longer produce tomatoes, the community response was overwhelming. We knew people liked our Hamakua Springs tomatoes, but none of us anticipated the number of comments we received, or the extent of them. It was really unbelievable.

One couple in Kailua on O'ahu wrote that they read about us stopping tomatoes due to our aging hydroponics houses with great dismay. They said they adored our tomatoes and would be very sad without them.

"I have a suggestion you may not have considered. I know that I would be more than willing to donate money towards a new system. I imagine that there are others who feel the same way we do and would do likewise. Is it worth your time to make a plea to the public for funds, stating the goal and having a chart indicating how close you are to that goal? Would the newspaper support your goal and put the information in a box on the front page, keeping track of the progress as well as keeping the public aware of your need? If there was a bank account or some such place to send funds, you might just receive enough to update your equipment and be back in the tomato business. It is so sad to see Hawaii become more dependent on imported food rather than less, as should be the goal."

It was a very generous idea, but I had to tell them that we'd passed the point of no return. The problem wasn't only that costs had increased, but that the energy that drives tomato production—the sun—had not.

When we started planning to diversify our business, oil cost $30 per barrel. Just five years later, oil cost more than $80 per barrel.

In terms of our hydroponic tomatoes, the pluses no longer exceeded the minuses.

Creating opportunities for our workers' kids

It's always been important to me to think not only about our business, but also how what we do affects our employees, our community, and the environment. Those aren't just words—I thought about that every time I made a decision. I was always thinking about the bigger picture; about how my choices affect things down the line. I still think that way.

I've always told politicians and business people, everybody, the same thing—that we know our workers didn't want their kids to be banana farm workers. Not that there's anything wrong with working on a banana farm. I always had tremendous respect for our employees, and still do. But we parents always want more for our kids.

That's why I push for economic development opportunities, and try to do whatever I can so the next generation will have more opportunities.

For instance, when the University of Hawai'i at Hilo was considering starting a school of pharmacy and was accepting testimony about it, I went and spoke in favor. I told them I wasn't there to support a school of pharmacy because it would help us sell more bananas. I was there because it meant more opportunities for our banana workers' kids.

Another example is the TMT on Mauna Kea. It provides economic opportunity for our island and our people. Some of our kids in the next generation might want to become astronomers, or otherwise work in that field.

That's my agenda. When I support something like the TMT, it's because I'm thinking about how it will help our workers and our island's people.

What it really comes down to is this: let's help our kids grow up to help themselves, so they don't have to leave Hawai'i to have a satisfying career and own a home, or end up needing subsidies from the state.

Chapter 10

The Oil Problem

Today, we're using less oil due to the COVID-19 pandemic, and so the price of oil is down. But that's temporary. In the background, world oil supplies continue to decline. We know that for the past twenty to thirty years we've been using two to three times more oil than we've been finding. As a result, oil is getting more and more expensive.

In the 1930s, you could pull 100 barrels of oil out of the ground with the energy from one barrel of oil. In the 1970s, that ratio had decreased 30:1, meaning the energy from one barrel of oil only got us 30 barrels of oil. A few years ago, it was estimated to be about 10:1.

We are nearing the time when we will have used up half of all the oil that exists. While the other half will still be in the ground, it will be increasingly hard to tap.

At some point, the demand for oil—by billions and billions of people who cannot wait to get in their car and drive to McDonalds—will exceed the ability to pump that oil.

We call that situation "peak oil."

When it finally dawns on all of us that our oil supplies will never increase, people will get frightened. But at that point, it will be too late.

We really need to act now.

We in Hawai'i are especially vulnerable to oil supply problems. In addition to the prospect of having to pay unsustainable fossil fuel costs in the future, we currently import more than 80 percent of our food. We meet most of our food needs in a way that's highly dependent on fossil fuels.

When I learned how serious our oil problem was, I went through the five stages of grief: denial, anger, bargaining, depression, and acceptance.

If we keep chasing after oil as the price rises, and keep at it long enough, we will end up like Rapa Nui (Easter Island), unable to sustain ourselves.

We all agree this is true. We only differ about how bad it will be.

Learning about peak oil

All this started coming together for me the first time I attended a peak oil conference. That was back in 2007, and then I attended for several more years, too.

For most of those years, I was the only person there from Hawai'i, which I found worrisome.

Although I didn't want the responsibility, I felt like it was my kuleana (responsibility) to report back to the people of Hawai'i Island because I was the only person from Hawai'i at most of those conferences. Since I'm not a scientist or engineer, though, I paid attention and determined who was credible.

That's where I learned about Professor Charles A. S. Hall and his theory of Energy Return on Investment (EROI), which ties economics in with our biophysical world. Sometimes called "energy return on energy invested," it's a systems approach that doesn't separate everything into its own silo, but instead takes everything into consideration together. I've since brought Charlie Hall here to speak about this at UH Hilo and UH Manoa.

EROI boils down to one basic concept: we must have net energy to survive.

This idea is discussed as an economic concept, but really it goes back to biology. Consider a rainbow trout swimming in a river and catching flies. At the end of the day, it has to have caught enough flies not only to survive, but also to reproduce.

It's the same for every animal, including us.

Look at cheetahs. They've got to be able to run down antelopes and rabbits and whatever they eat, while still having enough energy left over to reproduce and raise their young.

What's also crucial to understand is that it takes energy to get energy. We have to be able to use energy not only to access our source of energy—like using oil to operate the drills that take more oil out of the ground—but also have enough left over to power our society.

This concept applies to organisms, organizations, and civilizations—everything.

The energy it takes to obtain energy, minus the energy we use to get our food, equals our lifestyle. In other words, how much energy is left over determines how we live.

That's why it's so important for farmers to grow plenty of food. It means that others can do what they do and we can continue to have a vibrant society.

If farmers didn't plan ahead to provide enough food and, as a consequence, every family had to grow its own food, we would be a very different and much more limited society. People would not be able to pursue the arts, write books, or explore space. We would have way fewer choices.

Peak oil: not just fear-mongering

Frankly, there are a lot of alarmist websites about peak oil that sell books and videos about "the end of the world as we know it" and how to protect oneself. Looking at some of those websites, one could easily dismiss peak oil as something people made up to try to scare others and make a buck.

But that's not it. Peak oil is not at all merely some sort of alarmist nonsense.

It's nothing more than the fact that oil keeps getting more and more expensive and we have to figure out how to adapt.

I don't believe in doomsday scenarios like on those alarmist sites. I believe we can absolutely influence the course of events to come. We will adapt by carpooling, using clotheslines to dry our clothes, and catching our drinking water, for instance.

What I'm mostly concerned about as prices continue rising, though, is our most basic need—the ability to feed ourselves.

Before industrial agriculture, we relied on the sun for energy to grow our food; directly for the greens, and indirectly for the animals that ate the greens. Then came industrial agriculture, which relied on cheap oil, as low as $3 per barrel, to fuel its growth.

Now, as oil prices continue to rise, we are having to spend more and more of our income to buy food.

We hear people worrying about whether our energy is green, but that's not what's important right now. It's the price of the energy that matters. Higher-priced energy results in people having less discretionary income. We know this to be true in our gut.

The big question surrounding peak oil is when, exactly, the demand will permanently exceed supply. It used to be that the year 2030 seemed like a reasonable estimate. Some experts said that by 2030, we would need to discover the equivalent of four new Saudi Arabias just to keep up with the oil we need.

Now, more than a few people are saying peak oil could be sooner. Some are saying we may already be there.

It's not a question of whether or not we have oil reserves. There's a lot of oil in the ground. It's about whether we'll be able to replace expiring oil fields with new ones in a timely manner. Many experts feel that we won't be able to.

Furthermore, we don't even know how much of an oil reserve we have. There are indications that the OPEC producers don't have the reserves they say they do. We don't know for sure, because they won't show us proof.

So what will happen? Likely, prices will rise slowly and steadily as oil supplies decline. People will conserve energy as best they can by adjusting their behavior.

Because it is finite, though, sooner or later we will not be able to maintain the amount of oil we burn every day.

We will run out of the energy our society depends upon.

When shale oil came in it seemed, for a while, to have solved the problem. All of the sudden, there was a great big supply of oil from shale.

People claimed that the United States had one hundred years of natural gas available, accessible by using high water pressure to fracture the rocks where it was trapped. That's what "fracking" is.

Shale gas made a significant impact and we stopped talking about needing to import natural gas.

At one peak oil conference, I took a special interest in a panel that included the CEO of a gas drilling company and Arthur Berman, a geologist who analyzes gas wells.

Berman said he studied four thousand shale wells in the Barnett Shale in Texas and found that 90 percent of the total production of an average shale well was extracted in just four years. That meant you needed to drill a new well every four years just to stay even. It wasn't sustainable.

From about 2010, shale oil started increasing dramatically and unexpectedly, but it was not profitable and financing started drying up in 2018. Many shale companies went out of business.

It's unlikely we'll ever have such high levels of oil again in the United States.

COVID-19 is masking the longer-term problem, but that's only temporary. This problem has been coming for a long time and it's not going away—it's only going to get worse. We need to be working on this energy problem right now.

We must change our behavior.

We are so lucky here

Here on the Big Island, we are so fortunate. Sometimes we forget just how lucky we are.

My family was really poor when I was growing up at Waiākea Uka Camp 6. I don't think we ever had an extra blanket in the house. When I was in elementary school and it got really, really cold (like mid- to high-50 degrees) I remember going into the dresser drawer and throwing all the clothes on top of my blanket. No big deal.

When I attended the Association for the Study of Peak Oil & Gas USA conference in Houston one October, I was wearing what I always wear — shorts and a pullover shirt. I didn't have the heart to tell people I'd wear shorts throughout the entire winter, or that we would also be growing food all year long. I didn't tell them that in Hawai'i, we have a geothermal resource to provide us with energy but are reluctant to use it.

We all knew the consequence of rising oil prices in the coldest parts of the country. The others, going back to their homes elsewhere in the U.S., faced a very serious and even bleak future. I was going back to the Big Island, where we live amidst an embarrassment of rich natural resources. I just could not bring myself to tell them.

Chapter 11

We Teach Economics Completely Wrong

I'm also concerned that we are teaching our college students wrong. In economics, we teach that land, labor, and capital are the elements of production.

I'm not an economist, or an expert on the economy, but this just seems wrong to me.

Somewhere along the line, we forgot it was energy from cheap oil that made deploying capital possible. We started believing that growth was automatic, and that's what we have taught millions of students—that it's okay to rely on finite resources indefinitely.

Maybe this complex society we've built from cheap oil has become too complex to understand. Let's look at the history:

In the 1600s, wealthy people were those that owned lots of land. The sun was the energy that made things grow. So the more land you had, the more sun energy you had working for you. Makes sense.

In the 1700s, we started using metal tools to produce more food, and because society could feed more people, our population increased. The additional numbers worked in factories, and we also produced steam engines that created wealth. Okay, that's understandable. The Industrial Revolution came about and labor was an important factor of production. So far, so good.

Then, in the mid-1800s, we started using cheap oil, and over the next 150 years we built a very complex society. We needed to keep score and deploy resources and so we described that as "capital." And things got complex.

So what happens as oil declines? It seems to me the total amount of work people can do will also decline. What if, instead of four quarts of gas, you're sent out to cut down trees with your chainsaw and you only have three quarts? You'll probably produce fewer logs and be less productive. I think that is what we can expect to happen to our world's economy.

I truly believe the social science of economics has lost its way.

I wonder if we've already reached peak oil. If so, there's no better place to be than here in Hawai'i. We're fortunate to have abundant natural resources we can use to generate electricity. If we react in a smart way, we should be fine.

Food prices for goods shipped or flown in from afar will continue to rise. Are we in danger of starving to death? The answer is a resounding NO!

If the worse happened and ships only visited us intermittently (which isn't likely), we on the Big Island could grow what we need to feed ourselves. Piece of cake.

We have knowledgeable people at the universities and government agencies, as well as people who are knowledgeable in traditional ways. And the Big Island is sparsely populated with plenty of room to grow food.

We also have abundant water resources here on the Big Island. One inch of rain falling on one acre is equivalent to 27,000 gallons of water. The average rainfall at Pepe'ekeo, where we farmed, is 140 inches per year. That means in an average year, 3.7 million gallons of water falls on each acre. That means an amazing 2.2 billion gallons of rain fall on our 600 acres in an average year. Most of that runs into rivers and out to the ocean.

When we needed to think about what we can do to help O'ahu cope, we started leasing parts of our land to other farmers. Our objective was to get sufficient variety and volume of produce to make inter-island barge shipments economical and timely.

So we are not going to starve, freeze, or overheat. And if we choose, we can have clean, low-carbon-footprint jobs and energy production.

What more do we need?

We are also lucky here because we know that pre-contact Hawaiians sustained a population that was nearly the same size we have here today. They showed us it can be done. That knowledge, along with modern technology, means we should be able to produce enough food for this entire island if we put our minds to it and contribute to the needs of the rest of the state, too.

We need to engage youngsters—our next generation—at the earliest levels. We should frame the issue and pose the question to elementary schoolkids: "How can you help us feed Hawai'i?" I can see them jumping on their computers and proudly pointing out different methods that people in other parts of the world use to grow food.

That's become one of my missions—to make people aware that we need to address this issue, and show how it can be done. How all farmers—large and small, working together— can make Hawai'i self-sufficient in food once again.

We can do this!

Can!

Our edge: an abundance of natural resources

Hawai'i farmers already have an edge over mainland farmers because of sun energy. Our long summer days result in high production and, unlike many parts of the country, we have the advantage of sunlight throughout the entire year.

But we'd have an additional advantage if we could use our natural resources to produce cheaper electricity. Many folks think fuel is the highest cost of getting farm-grown food to the table. It is actually the cost of electricity, though. Keeping the cold chain from the farm to the home refrigerator is even more expensive than running the tractors.

We started looking into using the water that flows downstream at the farm to generate electricity. The farm has three streams and three springs, which is just a tremendous amount of water. It's because of all that water we were able to install a hydroelectric system. Water from an old plantation flume runs through the headworks, into a pipe, and then into a turbine, which is housed in a blue shipping container. A lone electric pole stands next to the system. That's the end of the line.

Or the start of the line, really, as that's where the electricity from the turbine goes. From there, it works its way across electric lines stretched between new poles that run across our farm land.

We started working on our hydroelectric project in 2009. It was a net metering project, meaning the meter would spin forward if we use electricity from Hawaii Electric Light Company (HELCO) and backwards when we supplied electricity to the utility company. We were able to supply all our own electrical needs and the farm used every bit of electricity we produced.

The EROI for hydro projects is estimated to be 84:1. That's a great return, and in fact hydroelectric has the highest EROI of electric power generation systems according to the journal

Energy Policy (Vol. 64, January 2014). We should definitely bring more Hamakua Coast hydroelectric plants online.

Our hydroelectric project was financed by the U.S. Department of Agriculture farm loan program. That's a legislative bill I initiated when I got back from the 2007 peak oil conference. It's a U.S. Department of Agriculture farm loan program just for renewable energy projects and it's still available to farmers.

The plan was to use our hydroelectric power to generate hydrogen. With that we could possibly make ammonia for fertilizer, and we speculated we could maybe even use it for running internal combustion engine farm equipment.

More changes at the farm

We also downsized our farm, and made up for the loss in production by leasing land to area farmers to grow crops like taro, corn, ginger, and sweet potato.

As a result of all that, our land's productivity actually improved and we increased the variety of products, as well. Another benefit was that it strengthened our community.

We also experimented with producing protein on the farm by raising tilapia in four blue pools we situated next to the reservoir. We put the pools at different heights so that gravity—rather than a pump—let the water flow from one pool to the next. Besides it being free, falling into the next pool oxygenated the water.

We didn't end up raising the fish commercially, although that was originally our goal, but gave them to our workers (along with vegetables) in lieu of monetary raises that we wanted but couldn't afford to give at the time.

Continuing to farm meant we were still providing food to the community, employing people locally, and making it possible for our people to stay in Hawai'i. This as opposed to people, or their children, having to leave the islands to make a decent lives for themselves.

Everything we did was geared toward keeping the farm economically viable and sustainable. I say it all the time: "If farmers make money, farmers will farm."

The hydroelectric system saved us thousands of dollars per month in electric bills and let us expand into other products and activities. It meant the farm stayed in business and provided for the surrounding community. It meant people had jobs.

That's the reason why, on a bigger scale, I have long advocated we use more geothermal energy on the Big Island. I want to lessen the stranglehold that high electricity costs have over us, so the rubbah slippah folk have breathing room and we all have more disposable income. That, in turn, will drive our local economy and make our islands more competitive with the rest of the world. It will also make our standard of living comparably higher.

Chapter 12

So What's the Answer?

I'm no scientist. I'm a farmer who's spent a lot of time dealing with the physical stuff out there in the rain and dirt. I come at this practically, always remembering my Pop's lesson: "Not no can, can!"

I'm always trying to find a solution to something or other by thinking hard and planning ahead. And that's what we need to be doing now. Contingency planning.

We need to take sustainable action now to prepare for a better future. And these actions have to be economically, environmentally, and socially sustainable.

As for the economic part, people understand what you need to do to make that work. Environmentally, too.

What's generally missing, and what I gravitate toward, is the social part of sustainability: leaving no one behind. I always come at everything from that point of view.

Here on the Big Island, we have the state's lowest median family income, a homelessness problem, and many other social ills. When I look at solutions, I want to make sure they address these problems.

As imported food prices rise, I believe local farming will become more profitable. That, and the proliferation of farmers markets, will make farming more sustainable. If farmers make money, farmers will farm.

We cannot wait for the public utilities to bring down energy costs. I trust individual farmers to do what they need to do. Think small-scale biodiesel. Other solutions include hydroelectric, windmills, and solar, to name just a few.

The more one farmer can produce, the more vibrant our society will be post-oil decline. We don't want to go back to where everyone has to fish or farm to feed their own family.

The key is how much help a farmer can get from alternate energy to assist with production.

It's interesting to look at what happened in Cuba and North Korea, both of which were dependent on oil supplies from the former Soviet Union. When that country collapsed, Cuba and North Korea suddenly had to fend for themselves.

In North Korea, there was widespread famine and crop failures.

Cuba plunged into a fuel and food crisis as well, and its average citizen's daily calorie intake declined from 2,600 in the late 1980s to only 1,000 to 1,500 calories in 1993.

But people began growing their own food, even in urban areas. They started co-ops to buy and sell produce. And by 2008, people were back to eating 2,600 calories per day. The country suffered for a generation but ultimately transitioned to a solid system of sustainable agriculture.

One basic difference was that Cuba has more energy from sunshine than North Korea.

I also think we can improve on the Cuba model.

Food security in Hawai'i

Here in Hawai'i, we use petroleum to generate more than 60 percent of our electricity. This is significantly higher than elsewhere in the country. So when the price of oil rises, we are impacted much more than are electricity customers on the mainland.

It's that expensive electricity that throttles our efforts to be food self-sufficient.

We all know that Hawai'i imports more than 80 percent of its food and there's only a seven-day food supply on the island at any one time.

Food security is about our farmers here in Hawai'i farming and producing our food. So why don't we just grow more here and stop importing so much food?

It's not as easy as that, actually. As the oil price rises, any mainland food product with electricity usage embedded in its production has a cost advantage over the same product being produced in Hawai'i. In other words, because we pay so much more for electricity, it costs a lot more to produce that food here in Hawai'i.

It's just much cheaper to import it. That's true whether we're talking about ice cream, bakery products, or jams and jellies.

Another example is modern poultry production. To maximize egg production, you need constant electric lighting. And we automate feeding chickens and collecting eggs by using long conveyor belts that run on electricity. We use electric motors and conveyor belts to clean and sort eggs. Eggs go into temperature-controlled rooms, which we keep cool with electric motors.

It's hard for our local egg producers to compete here in Hawai'i, where we depend on ever-more-expensive oil for electricity much more than the mainland does. We end up buying mainland eggs because they are so much cheaper than eggs produced here.

And so Hawai'i becomes even less food secure.

Our expensive electricity here in Hawai'i also makes it hard for small farmers to refrigerate their produce. That's why people complain that locally grown produce doesn't last as long as produce that's grown elsewhere. Not only does the product break down faster, but that can also affect food safety.

It doesn't have anything to do with how the farmer grows the produce, but everything to do with the cost of the electricity needed to preserve the product.

And that's not even the most energy-intensive part of food production. What uses the most energy is the temperature-controlled supply chain needed to preserve the food as it goes from the farm to the wholesaler and retailer along the way to getting to your refrigerator.

Wander around KTA or any other supermarket and you'll see so many products that are affected by high electricity costs. A grocery store itself has to be air-conditioned. It has to have refrigerated cases and rotisseries, as well as refrigerated milk, meat, and produce coolers in the back.

Of course, supply chains and grocery stores on the U.S. mainland use a similar amount of electricity. But we pay so much more for that electricity all along the way that we really notice it in our food costs. As the price of oil goes up and electricity costs rise, so do the prices of our locally produced food.

Farmers are price-takers, not price-makers. So when the fossil fuel or biofuel oil price rises, and it becomes more expensive to produce products, farmers cannot pass on their higher costs to the consumer.

That's the bottom line about Hawai'i being food-sufficient: we must make it more affordable for farmers to produce their food crops. They have to be able to earn a decent living, or they'll do something else. Unfortunately, we can already see that farmers are getting older. Our younger generations are not going into agriculture.

So as we look for solutions to our oil dependence, we must also consider the solution cost because that will completely impact our food security and ability to be self-sufficient.

So what's the answer? Cheap electricity.

On the Big Island, that means geothermal electricity. As the cost of exporting food across the ocean to Hawai'i continues to rise, our local farmers will greatly benefit from lower, stable electricity costs generated by geothermal energy.

The more geothermal we use to generate electricity, and the less fossil or biofuel oil we use, the more food-secure Hawai'i Island will be.

There's hope

Although oil is becoming more scarce, and imported food prices are increasing, I believe the situation is hopeful. We can:

- Landscape by growing plants that make food. Garden wherever possible and plant fruit trees. 'Ulu trees come to mind, because they provide such an abundant supply of the tasty starch food.

- Get to know our neighbors, plan what we can trade, and get closer to our families. Kids can have chores taking care of the plants. That is not a bad thing. In my family, we kids fed the chickens before we went to school.

We can do this.

Hawai'i's "2050 Sustainability Plan: Charting a Course for the Decade of Action" should have food as its top priority. One thing we need is to do an assessment of the number and composition of calories necessary to maintain a population of 1.5 million.

Andrew Hashimoto, dean of the University of Hawai'i College of Tropical Agriculture and Human Resources, mentioned it's something like two billion calories per year.

We should compare the number of needed calories with what we can provide now—how many calories' worth of food we grow in Hawai'i at present—in terms of human nutrition. That will give us a road map to follow.

I am optimistic that we can successfully achieve these goals and demonstrate to the rest of the nation how to take care of each other with aloha.

It's by forcing change that we will achieve food and economic security for this island. It's about starting now so we have time to transition to a better and more sustainable future that improves our lives here on the Big Island, and makes this a better home for our children and grandchildren.

It's not random that I'm such a supporter of Big Island issues like geothermal energy and the TMT. I knew this issue was so serious that I needed to bring it back to Hawai'i.

I also knew I wouldn't be credible or effective if I let myself get involved in anything that could be perceived as a conflict of interest. That's why, early on, I decided I'd never hire out as a consultant or invest in any energy issues. I don't have any financial interest whatsoever in either geothermal or the TMT.

But both are directly related to what's happening on our island and in our world.

They will help us as we deal with the situation that is peak oil, and its huge and detrimental effects on being able to provide our people with affordable food.

I believe there's time to adjust, but, for the sake of our people, we just cannot afford to waste the opportunities available to us.

Part 3

The Solutions

There are three different but related ways we can bring together culture and science here on Hawai'i Island to make a better life—both for us now and for the generations to come.

I've been talking about all this for many years, but it turns out Papakū Makawalu was the missing puzzle piece. When I started learning about that, I finally understood how it all truly fits together.

Papakū Makawalu is a methodology for teaching and understanding Hawaiian culture, including Hawaiian knowledge and values. It's clearly visible in the Hawaiian creation chant, the *Kumulipo*, and the Edith Kanaka'ole Foundation (EKF) is currently revitalizing it. I've been learning about it in a class with EKF's Kekuki Keali'ikanaka'ole, and it's fascinating.

You probably know that the *Kumulipo* describes the sea, land, earth, and stars. The Papa Hānau Moku section of the chant is a genealogy of all living plants and animals. As a farmer, that's my favorite of the Papakū Makawalu's three parts.

The other two parts are Papa Huli Lani, which is about the skies, and Papa Huli Honua, about the earth.

Despite living without fossil fuels, our early Hawaiian ancestors managed very well. They had their own perspectives on science that determined how they understand and used it, and they created a great environment and society for themselves. They thrived. There's a lot we can study and learn about from how they lived.

Fortunately, there's a lot we can do.

1. Siting the TMT on Hawai'i Island, known as the best place in the world for world-class astronomy, will let us look deep into and learn more about pō, the darkness, just as the *Kumulipo* describes.

2. Creating a significant Hawaiian culture and science center above the clouds will give us an important location where Hawaiians can gather to practice, evolve, and pass on cultural knowledge and astronomy.

3. Assessing and tapping into geothermal energy away from the active East Rift Zone will provide the affordable, firm, and stable electrical power, hydrogen, and other resources that our island needs.

Chapter 13

The Thirty Meter Telescope

Placing the new, unique, and very advanced TMT on Maunakea means many things for us here in Hawai'i.

First, it's an enormous move forward for science. It's a once-in-a-lifetime chance to do something this huge and vital and an opportunity to help lift up and educate our keiki and future generations. It's a much-needed beacon of light shining at our often-overlooked native Hawaiian community and culture. The telescope will also provide many with a safe, steady income and help stabilize our economy.

Here's how the TMT organization defines the telescope:

> A new class of extremely large telescopes that will allow us to see deeper into space and observe cosmic objects with unprecedented sensitivity. With its 30m prime mirror diameter, TMT will be three times as wide, with nine times more area, than the largest currently existing visible-light telescope in the world. This will provide unparalleled resolution with TMT images more than 12 times sharper than those from the Hubble Space

Telescope. When operational, TMT will provide new observational opportunities in essentially every field of astronomy and astrophysics. Observing in wavelengths ranging from the ultraviolet to the mid-infrared, this unique instrument will allow astronomers to address fundamental questions in astronomy ranging from understanding star and planet formation to unraveling the history of galaxies and the development of large-scale structure in the universe.

The telescope is being designed and developed by an international, nonprofit partnership between the California Institute of Technology, the University of California, the National Institutes of Natural Sciences of Japan, the National Astronomical Observatories of the Chinese Academy of Sciences, the Department of Science & Technology of India, and the National Research Council Canada.

Why situate it on Maunakea? Because the TMT board conducted an intense, five-year global search for the optimum place to locate the telescope, measuring virtually every atmospheric feature that could affect its performance. They found that Maunakea is the best place in the entire world for this amazing new type of telescope.

In the world! Imagine that.

It's really something that our beloved mountain, which has historically been a beacon for Hawai'i's own explorers and navigators of the stars and sea, will now be a beacon for another realm. It will still allow us to study the stars, but now we will also be able to explore beyond. It's huge.

Backlash

There's been a backlash against the idea of locating the TMT on Maunakea. A small but vocal group of Hawaiians and their supporters say that Maunakea already has too many telescopes.

They call the mountain a sacred and delicate site, and say the University of Hawai'i, which manages the astronomical area, has mismanaged it for decades.

They have physically blocked access, filed numerous court cases about construction permits, and even interrupted the TMT's groundbreaking ceremony in 2014.

Although the TMT board selected the telescope location in close consultation with native Hawaiians in order to avoid areas of cultural or archaeological concern, protestors call the entire mountain culturally significant. They say the telescope is an eyesore and inappropriate.

But there's been a great deal of support, including among native Hawaiians, from the beginning. When we had our first sign-waving in support of the TMT, nearly 150 people showed up. We told everyone we were meeting to celebrate the process and told them to bring their kids, and they did. It was very significant.

While the anti-TMT people are vocal, there's a large, much more silent majority of the public that supports the project. A 2020 Ward Research public opinion poll found that 61 percent of Hawai'i residents support moving ahead with construction, and 32 percent are opposed.

I've been in the middle of this TMT issue for a very long time now, and I've seen the shift in public opinion. Many people come forward, consistently, to thank us for supporting the TMT. They are afraid to express their support publicly because the subject has become so volatile.

My role now is support. I can see more and more young people starting to come out in support of the TMT and its opportunities for a better future, and I could not be more pleased.

Benefitting future generations

The knowledge that such an advanced telescope can give us about space and our place in it is immense.

The fact that Maunakea was identified as the single best place in the world for such astronomical research fits completely with how significant our ancestors found it for studying the stars. It's an honor for Hawai'i.

And it means that not only can Hawai'i contribute to the world's understanding of astronomy, but the islands can also provide opportunities for those in future generations who want to learn about the stars as their ancestors did. We need to keep providing avenues for our keiki and the children yet to come so they have every advantage.

Chad Kalepa Baybayan said it perfectly: "I firmly believe the highest level of desecration rests in actions that remove the opportunity and choices from the kind of future our youth can own." I strongly agree with that.

Kalepa was a master navigator and navigator-in-residence at 'Imiloa Astronomy Center, and a graduate of the Hawaiian language college at UH Hilo.

When I look at him, I see a thousand years of our history, and because of his science, a thousand years of our future, too.

Unfortunately, he passed away far too soon, in 2021. It was an enormous loss.

He sure left behind a lot of wisdom, though. For example, in a *West Hawaii Today* newspaper article, he reminded us about our forebearers:

> As explorers, Hawaiians utilized island resources to sustain their communities. ...They ventured to Mauna Kea, reshaped the environment by quarrying rock, left behind evidence of their work, and took materials off the mountain to serve their communities with the full consent and in the presence of their gods.

And he wrote about why the TMT will be such a benefit to Hawai'i and its people:

> When it is completed, the Thirty Meter Telescope on Mauna Kea will, with greater accuracy and speed, vastly increase the capacity for the kind of scientific research vital to the quest for mankind's future. It takes place on a sacred mountain; remains consistent with the work of our ancestral forebears; and is done to the benefit of tomorrow's generations, here in Hawaii and across the globe.

I truly agree with everything he felt and expressed. He was such a wise man and so well-respected.

His funeral was the most impressive such gathering I ever experienced. When they flew his body home from O'ahu, the mortuary picked him up at Hilo Airport. As the hearse drove past the Civil Air Patrol at the airport, it stopped for a huge crowd of people who had gathered to pay their respects. Open-ocean sailors and navigators, family, and friends.

So many people respected him. I hope those people will consider his wisdom and words about the TMT when they remember him.

At that visitation at the airport, when it was my turn to pay respects at the hearse, I put a tightly clenched fist down gently on the coffin. I felt very determined, and my teeth were clenched. I told Kalepa, "We not going quit."

Respecting the process

The TMT is a once-in-a-lifetime opportunity for us to make wise decisions and help our future generations. If we bring the new telescope here, we have an excellent opportunity to negotiate educational opportunities for our keiki and create jobs for our families.

But we must make sure everything is pono (in perfect order) first. When the process is pono, and we aloha everyone on all sides of the issue, then we're good.

We do this by having respect for each other, Hawaiian style, and respecting the process.

Patrick Kahawaiola'a is president of the Keaukaha Community Association, and we've talked story in the community a lot. Many years ago he taught me how critical the process is as people work through differences, and I've always remembered that. It definitely applies to the TMT. It makes so much sense to me.

When the process is the most critical factor in a discussion, all contributors to the process—no matter what side of the issue—make for a better result. Regarding the TMT, we always kept in mind that we need to aloha the loud voices, too, the ones that told us things were not quite right early on.

It is always about all of us. Not me against you. Therefore, we must mahalo Kealoha, Lanakila, Nelson, Debbie, Paul, Ku, Hanalei, the Kanaka Council, Jim, Cory, Moani, and many others. We would not be here today had it not been for their passionate advocacy.

The TMT folks, led by Henry Yang, have done it the right way. Our approach is based on mutual respect, collaboration, and trust. It wouldn't have worked any other way.

The whole state has noticed that we on the Big Island are doing this differently. It truly does boil down to the process.

Education is the game-changer

A huge reason I'm such a firm believer in the TMT is because of what it offers our keiki regarding education.

Keiki education is the common denominator that everyone, on all sides of the issue, can agree upon. That's how the THINK fund was born. The TMT folks pledged $1 million annually to the newly created THINK fund for fifty years. That's $50 million coming to our island that is earmarked solely for our kids' education.

It will not be administered by the state Department of Education but by carefully selected community members, primarily for K-12 education. I see it as a way of opening up kids' minds and helping them understand that they can do anything.

Education is directly related to family income, and it's a game-changer. The more education, the higher the family income. That's pretty well understood and not that complex.

According to Statista, the 2019 median family income in the state of Hawai'i was $88,006. Here on the Big Island, it was only $62,409. And on the east side of the Big Island, it's much lower than that.

We all know that low family income is sometimes associated with societal problems. And, unfortunately, it's true that Hawaiian families occupy the lowest rungs on the family income ladder.

Here's the key: education is the great equalizer.

We have a lot of problems on this island, and education can make a big difference. Not only are education and family income linked, but both have a substantial impact on other social issues, too. Making positive changes to our educational offerings would help raise everybody up.

We don't want our kids to wallow in victim-ism. That is *waste time*. We need them to take pride in knowing that their ancestors were smart and strong—astronomers and the best navigators in the world. We need them to know their worth and be optimistic. We need them to have hopes and dreams and work toward strong futures.

We want this TMT fund to help prepare students to succeed. So many of our Big Island kids don't go on to college. Of the ones that do, far too many don't stay the course and graduate.

If we are truly interested in elevating our people and helping them rise above drug problems, abusive relationships, and other social ills, we must help parents launch their kids into the middle class. We want all our island's kids to believe that high aspirations and goals are not out of the ordinary but the norm.

For those who are prepared to succeed, the sky's the limit.

Perpetuating Unique Educational Opportunities (PUEO)

Some years ago, several of us formed the 501(c)(3) nonprofit group PUEO to further "educational opportunities for the children of Hawai'i in the fields of science, technology, engineering, and mathematics." PUEO stands for Perpetuating Unique Educational Opportunities, and we started it to help our kids.

Keahi Warfield is the perfect leader for PUEO. I'll always do everything I can to support his efforts.

PUEO was allowed to participate in the TMT contested case hearing in 2016. The contested case hearing resulted from a Hawai'i Supreme Court ruling on the TMT's 2011 conservation district use permit. The court ruled that the Board of Land and Natural Resources should not have approved the permit before hearing all evidence.

Our group felt compelled to participate because of the impact the decision would have on future generations. We also want the discussions to include keiki education. Being allowed to participate meant ensuring a more robust and better-rounded discussion of the issues.

Kalepa Baybayan was also on the PUEO Board. He felt so strongly about the TMT he flew up from the South Pacific to testify at the contested case hearing, and then flew back to where he was taking place in the worldwide voyage of the traditional Polynesian canoes Hōkūle'a and Hikianalia. That's how determined and dedicated he was.

But PUEO didn't merely spring up to argue for the TMT, as some mistakenly claimed. On the contrary, many of us on the PUEO Board of Directors have been involved in promoting educational opportunities for our island's children for a very long time.

Back in 2007, for instance, a couple of us started the Adopt-A-Class program when we learned elementary school students in Keaukaha didn't go on field trips because the school couldn't afford it. We asked people to sponsor individual classes at Keaukaha Elementary School and ended up paying for buses and entry fees for each class to visit 'Imiloa Astronomy Center every semester.

'Imiloa is a compelling choice because it situates the Hawaiian culture and scientific knowledge in parity with the highest level of astronomy. It's a "discovery center" that celebrates both science (the world-class astronomy atop nearby Maunakea) and Hawaiian culture (including the genius of traditional Hawaiian voyaging, navigation, and much more).

The idea was to send our Keaukaha kids on annual excursions that broaden their horizons, help them develop an excitement for learning, and create positive attitudes about their place in the world. It's my opinion that if Hawaiian kids are comfortable with their place in the world, they will not hesitate to participate in that world.

At 'Imiloa, Hawaiian kids see there are careers and avocations directly related to their culture. They realize these cultural traditions are important enough to be celebrated in a world-class museum. And that the people pursuing these careers and passions look just like them and their families.

After a while, the Gordon and Betty Moore Foundation expanded the Adopt-A-Class program to cover every class on the Big Island—in public, private, and charter schools. This is an ongoing, impactful, and lasting program that's still sending every Hawai'i Island school student to 'Imiloa every year.

'What about the rest?'

Another impetus for formally creating the nonprofit organization PUEO was an exchange I had with Lehua Veincent, who was then the Keaukaha Elementary School principal (these days he's the high school principal at Kamehameha Schools Hawai'i).

Many years back, I asked him what he felt the TMT should offer the Big Island as an introductory, good faith gift. I asked him if it would be appropriate to ask for "full-ride" scholarships for at least five native Hawaiians to attend the nation's best colleges.

He asked me, very sincerely, "And what about the rest?"

I felt so stupid that I could feel my ears getting hot.

That's the quintessential question. "What about the rest?" It's about the keiki, the future generations—all of them.

That discussion I had with Kumu Lehua changed everything.

Three years later, University of Hawai'i President McClain announced the $50 million benefits package for education. That came about directly as a result of Kumu Lehua's question: "What about the rest?"

PUEO is made up of very credible native Hawaiian people. In all my years of knowing them, it's always been about community, keiki, and our future generations. I'm very proud to be able to work with these people.

Henry Yang, chancellor of the University of California at Santa Barbara, is president of the TMT Board, and I've gotten to know him well over the years. I'm very impressed with him.

He and Jean-Lou Chameau, president emeritus of Cal Tech, visited the Big Island countless times in the early years to advocate for the TMT. They understood that the common denominator on which people on all sides of the issue could agree was the education of our keiki.

Henry and Jean-Lou listened to our advice early on. They went and talked to community folks, like Kumu Lehua and Patrick Kahawaiola'a, and truly listened. As a result, they became well-known in the community.

One visit to Keaukaha was memorable. They dropped in unexpectedly at a Kūpuna Day function. They'd become so familiar that people greeted them with, "Come, come, come, go eat."

In 2015, I was at The Queen's Medical Center in Honolulu for a triple bypass and valve replacement. June and Tracy were still sitting in the waiting room where they'd been sitting for hours, waiting to hear from a doctor, when they looked up and saw Henry walking down the hallway toward them, chatting with a nurse. Henry told June and Tracy what was going on and that I was going to be all right.

He'd arrived at the hospital, said he was a relative, and talked his way into my ICU room. I was out and don't remember him being there, but later, he told me I was hooked up to a lot of tubes, and that he checked out my vital signs and saw they looked fine.

It made me laugh to hear that he did that. He said he just wanted to have a look and make sure I was doing okay.

I could tell from the first time I met Henry that he was a good guy. Trustworthy. Caring. Someone you can do business with on a handshake.

That's rare.

I feel so strongly that we need to create more and better opportunities for our young people. That way, when they grow up, they won't have to leave the Islands to create a successful life for themselves and their families.

It convinces me that the $1 million annual TMT contribution toward the Big Island's K-12 education will be valuable to our children. It's no longer about us—now it's about the future generations.

You know how we'll know that we've done our job? When our keiki have the values and skills they need to create a society that's successful when they need to fend for themselves, whether figuratively or literally. When they are able to thrive even "when the boat no come."

We must learn and perpetuate the knowledge and skills that allowed Hawaiians to survive for hundreds of years out here in the middle of the ocean without boats arriving every day with goods from someplace else.

In the future, our values will also need to revolve around aloha. We need to make more friends and stay closer to our families. We need to continue helping each other. We need to assume kuleana.

Here in this modern world, how do we use what we have and meld it with the values that always worked for us? We need a balance of science and culture so we can work together to help our greater society.

I remember what my Pop told me: "There are a thousand reasons why 'No can.' I only looking for one reason why 'Can.'"

Center above the clouds

Another current project is to create "Mauna Honua: A Culture and Science Center Above the Clouds." It was Kalepa who proposed the name Mauna Honua.

Mauna Honua would be located on Maunakea, not at the summit but at a mid-level site that we hope the Department of Land and Natural Resources (DLNR) will turn over for the center.

Right now, there's no place on the mountain that represents Hawaiian values, culture, tradition, or thinking. All that's up there are telescopes, standing like massive temples.

Why aren't Hawaiians represented on the mountain? Why don't Hawaiians have a space there?

We aren't talking about a small space the size of your garage, as an afterthought. The Culture and Science Center Above the Clouds would present Maunakea as a quality place of high science and culture. It would mean additional respect for our people, our mountain, and our culture.

We're talking about a thoughtfully designed center that's large enough for meaningful work. It would be a place where present and future generations of Hawaiians could do their research and practice cultural preservation, education, language, science, and ecology.

It would be substantial so that when you visit, you know it represents the mountain—that the mountain is respected. It would be a pipeline from the university and community college's Hawaiian language and Hawaiian culture programs. Visitors from around the world would pay money to the center to visit and learn what we want to teach them.

The center would be a foundation, a papakū. The makawalu would be the Hawaiian culture and science "seeds," nourished there to spread around the world.

There are so many ideas about how to set up the center. Maybe you lessen car traffic up the mountain by running a ski lift and charging a hefty amount to ride it. Perhaps the lift uses electricity to run uphill but generates its own electricity as it goes back down the mountain.

The center as a whole would, fittingly for the mountain, use smart science. It would help us brand Hawai'i as a place of top-level science and quality—which is what the TMT represents. It would be a bold move toward rebranding our islands, now overly dependent on tourism, and diversifying our economy.

If we can come together, I'm pretty confident the will exists to gather the money for building the center. We wouldn't have to look to the university for it.

But we would have to work together to get such a culture center built. All of us, including Hawaiians, to create something that really works for our people, our culture, our goals, our future. We could do it together to benefit today's Hawaiians and future generations, too.

Chapter 14

The Gift of Geothermal

The energy model we're using now is not the smartest one for what's coming. We all need to get together and pull in the same direction.

More and more families cannot afford to live here any longer; in fact, more Hawaiians now live outside Hawai'i than live on these islands.

Isn't that the same as losing our land?

What are we doing about that?

There are going to be tough years ahead in terms of this energy crisis. It will impact us all dramatically, and we need to start figuring out our best scenarios.

Here in Hawai'i, we are unbelievably lucky to have a geothermal resource sitting beneath us at so many locations around the island. We are really fortunate to have geothermal, which many of us Hawaiians consider a gift from Pele, the goddess of volcanoes and fire. According to geologists, Hawai'i Island will be over the "hot spot" that creates our geothermal resource for

500,000 to one million years. It's a solution they don't have on the mainland.

When we use geothermal, our energy costs won't change. We won't be impacted by dramatically increasing costs rolling through our economy because of what's happening in other countries, as we are now.

But it will all depend on how much of our electricity is generated by geothermal. If it's just a small percentage, we will still be vulnerable to being shaken up pretty badly. If it's a large percentage, much less so.

There's been a significant change in how the native Hawaiian community perceives geothermal, especially compared to the 1970s, when geothermal was handled in a heavy-handed and "top-down" manner. Much safer production methods have replaced the technology that existed in the 1970s. Puna Geothermal Venture has been in operation for many years now as a good neighbor, and choosing geothermal energy is common sense.

With much cheaper geothermal energy as our source of power, customers would have more discretionary income to spend, businesses would flourish, and more people would have jobs. Folks would be able to take good care of their families. More Hawaiians would be able to raise their families here in Hawai'i.

Geothermal power beneath Hawaiian Home Lands

There have been some incredible, geothermal-related discoveries right on Hawaiian Home Lands properties.

While doing exploratory drilling for water at Pōhakuloa, for instance, they hit boiling water at the 6,000-foot level. Boiling water! And, interestingly, that heat was not associated with a rift zone.

Also, when doing surface exploration, they found hot rocks on Hawaiian Home Lands around Humu'ula. That geothermal resource may be larger than the entire east rift zone.

Since the Department of Hawaiian Home Lands (DHHL) owns the geothermal resource beneath its lands, it doesn't have to pay royalties for it.

It should map the sites and contract out energy production to the highest bidder.

Part of the rents and royalties paid could go to the native Hawaiian people, upon whose land it sits. That could mean beneficiaries receive regular monthly or yearly cash payments for a portion of the development. Something like the Alaska Permanent Fund Corporation, which pays Alaska citizens dividends every year based on earnings from the state's oil revenues.

The details would be up to DHHL and the beneficiaries to figure out. But it would mean that the more geothermal output we use, the more revenue from royalties we generate for native Hawaiians.

Hawaiians should act quickly to put this in place, or the power generation will be developed somewhere else, away from Hawaiian Home Lands, and they will not benefit from it.

Geothermal and its energy return on investment

Geothermal breaks even at the equivalent of $57 per barrel of oil.

As of November 2021, the oil price was $80 per barrel. There's volatility to the price of oil, and therefore to the cost of energy, that we won't have if we use geothermal energy.

Professor Charles A. S. Hall, of State University of New York, is the leading expert on energy return on investment (EROI) analysis. He estimates that we need a minimum EROI of 3:1 to maintain a sustainable society. Geothermal would put us way above that.

When I asked David Murphy, assistant professor of environmental studies at St. Lawrence University and author of the book *Energy Return on Investment*, about the EROI for geothermal, he estimated it's around 10:1.

And unlike the EROI for fossil fuels, which will steadily decrease, geothermal's EROI won't change for centuries because that's how long we will sit over the hot spot.

Compare geothermal's excellent EROI to oil conditions in Ghawar, Saudi Arabia, which will be unaffordable within one hundred years. The Permian Basin, an oil- and gas-producing area in the southwestern United States and the most prolific "sweet spot" in the shale patch, will likely be unaffordable in much less than fifty years.

I mentioned to David Murphy that very few places in the world are lucky enough to have a geothermal resource, and he agreed it's a very attractive alternative energy for Hawai'i to pursue. That's been the consensus of everyone I ask about geothermal. It's a no-brainer because geothermal costs remain stable.

There's a lot to like about geothermal energy and we must move toward it now. We can't wait. It's possible our economic system will be hit very hard in less than ten years. We don't know, but it's better to be prepared for the worst and hope for the best. No harm, no foul.

What will our grandkids and their kids think of us later if we don't do this now, while we can, and their lives are the worse for it?

Helping our people with low energy costs

I was part of the Geothermal Working Group, a County of Hawai'i-funded group that evaluated geothermal's potential as the county's primary energy source of electricity. We found some great advantages.

- Geothermal is an indigenous resource
- It costs less than half of what any other renewable energy alternatives costs
- It provides stable power
- It generates revenue for the state
- It creates community benefits
- It will be available for the 500,000 to one million years the Big Island is over the geothermal "hot spot"

In modern Hawaiian history, the culture has given, given, given and the economy has taken, taken, taken. But now we have a unique opportunity to turn that completely on its head. Now, the economy can provide (through the geothermal resource), and the culture can receive (affordable energy and all the benefits that brings).

If we can stabilize our energy costs so they stay inexpensive—which geothermal will let us do—we'll find that as the price of oil rises, we'll be more competitive with the rest of the world. As a result, our people's standard of living will improve. We'll be addressing the energy problem and taking care of the "rubbah slippah" folks, too.

Using geothermal for our energy will let us protect folks—forever—from ever-higher electricity and water bills and the other cost increases we can 100 percent expect from rising oil prices.

Otherwise, here's what will happen. Our electricity and water costs will rise and rise. The poorest among us may even have their electricity and water turned off at some point. People may start leaving the electric grid. At some point, schools might not be able to afford the electric rates, and they might have to turn off their air conditioning. Our children would have a more challenging time learning.

If we go the geothermal route, though, the grass will always be green. Our electricity and water costs will stay the same for centuries. After a while, our everyday living costs will be cheaper than what people are paying on the mainland.

Because our low-income folks would have extra money to spend locally, businesses would grow. And as our electricity costs became lower relative to prices on the U.S. mainland, we would be more competitive in manufacturing and other work that requires energy. Most of us would be cruising around in electric cars.

Although airfares may be very high, once visitors arrived here they would find our geothermal-powered location relatively cheaper than other vacation destinations. So while we could probably anticipate fewer tourists, those who came would probably stay longer and spend more money. That's definitely a win-win.

I can imagine those visitors would engage with the community in agricultural and other special experiences. I can see many more opportunities for our folks to interact with visitors and offer custom services.

It may be an opportunity for more individual entrepreneurs than we have in our current model of tourism. The government would see fewer folks fall through the cracks.

In so many ways, geothermal can help elevate all of us in terms of standard of living. If we plan well for our future, respectfully engaging with each other, I can see our greatest asset, our aloha, flourishing. And that, more than money, is what will make us all rich. As Pop used to say: "Not 'no can.' 'CAN!'"

Geothermal and base power

Base power, or base load energy, is the amount of power our electric utility needs to meet minimum customer demands and keep our lights from flickering. Base power is not only important for delivering dependable service, but it's also what has the most significant impact on our electricity bills.

Geothermal is by far the most affordable base power source. It's stable, a proven technology, and environmentally friendly. It gives off no greenhouse gases and has a small footprint compared to solar and biofuels.

It's in the best interest of both utility customers and the electric utility's stockholders that the utility switches to geothermal, providing a stabilizing force for electricity generation and protecting us from high oil prices. As the price of oil rises, we can shut down the much more expensive oil-fired generating plants. Homelessness will decrease, and businesses and jobs will grow. Our standard of living will increase relative to the rest of the world.

While there is no low-cost solution for generating base power on O'ahu, we can run a cable from the Big Island and use it to send them base power. They can supplement it with solar and wind. Otherwise, O'ahu will remain hopelessly dependent on oil.

Running cables between islands is doable. Unlike what some seem to think, it doesn't begin to approach the difficulty of flying to the moon. It can be done.

I firmly believe that, in close consultation with the Hawaiian community, we should consider using geothermal for most of the Big Island's electrical base power needs. It's the people on the lowest rungs of the economic ladder whose lights are turned off first. We must take care of the most defenseless among us. If they're safe, we're all safe.

Geothermal energy can create hydrogen

Hydrogen is one of the fastest-growing clean energy technologies. And in addition to geothermal generating electricity, it can also be used to produce hydrogen.

Hydrogen can be used as transportation fuel, heat for industrial processes and living spaces, and electric storage systems. Hydrogen eliminates pollution caused by fossil fuels, greenhouse gases and, of course, it means we're not dependent on the Middle East and its dwindling oil reserves. If you're interested, go read more about the "hydrogen economy."

More than 90 percent of all the hydrogen produced in the United States comes from natural gas, a finite resource. But here in Hawai'i, we can create hydrogen from unused geothermal energy produced in off-peak times that would otherwise go to waste.

We know that hydrogen works as a transportation fuel for gas and diesel engines. It can be moved and stored using similar infrastructure as propane. So our off-peak geothermal power can be used to make hydrogen for internal combustion engines, which we'll use in the future to run our cars and trucks. This will protect us from gasoline costs when people start buying more electric vehicles.

If hydrogen can be used in regular car engines, could ammonia be used to generate electricity in the electric utilities' diesel engines?

A lot of electric utilities create hydrogen by using natural gas. First, they buy the natural gas, which costs money. Then they remove the carbon, a process that costs more money and leaves a carbon leftover they have to get rid of.

In contrast, here's how to make hydrogen from geothermal energy: you just run the electricity through water, and that gives you hydrogen and oxygen.

Clearly, it will get more expensive to make hydrogen from natural gas as the supply of natural gas decreases. But producing hydrogen from geothermal energy here in Hawai'i will give us an advantage over time because the geothermal cost won't go up. The energy cost will remain the same.

And being able to produce hydrogen from geothermal means that as time goes on, Hawai'i will have an edge in terms of green, hydrogen-based products.

Another bonus is that we can use off-peak geothermal power to make ammonia, which can be used to create nitrogen. Our bodies need nitrogen. During a thunderstorm, electrical energy in lightning separates nitrogen atoms in the air. They fall to earth with rain and combine with minerals in the soil to form nitrates, which fertilizes the soil. We take that in through the plants we eat or by eating animals that eat those plants.

Geothermal does essentially the same thing as lightning. With geothermal, the earth's heat spins a turbine to create electricity and separate the nitrogen molecules.

Lighting is a natural process. Why not do the same thing using science? We can take electricity and make hydrogen and ammonia from the hydrogen. You end up with the same ammonia fertilizer. What's the difference?

As a farmer, I'm concerned about where we will get fertilizer because it keeps getting more expensive. Currently, we produce it by extracting nitrogen from the air and using high heat and pressure using oil and gas. The process requires a lot of energy.

But if oil and gas prices rise enough, we can substitute geothermal power. It's another way we can place ourselves in a position to win.

Because we are heavily reliant on oil, Hawai'i may be the canary in the coal mine for the rest of the country, and that's not good. In warning others of impending danger, the canary dies.

We don't want to serve as a warning to others; we want Hawai'i to be a beacon that shows the rest of the world how to create a better future.

We can start by taking a triple-bottom-line approach to the energy problems ahead of us. We need to put our people's needs first, consider the effects of any solutions on the environment, and make sure our energy investments make sense.

After all, it's not the strongest who survive. It's the ones who adapt.

Can you imagine it? Most of the state's electricity needs being powered by the Big Island's geothermal wells? Rents and royalties going to native Hawaiian people, and all of us being free from oil from the Middle East? It's a long-term solution that would serve us very well.

Alternative to biofuels

Here in Hawai'i, we've been focusing on trying to replace fossil fuel oil with biofuels. But when the replacement is just as expensive as oil—as is biofuel for electricity generation—that doesn't solve the problem.

Biofuel is a liquid fuel made from biomass, which is any plant or animal material used to produce electricity. One example of biomass is taking used vegetable oil from a restaurant and processing that into a biofuel. Making biofuel from waste oil works.

But it's proving to be very difficult to grow crops primarily for biofuels.

And there's an issue of scalability in terms of going from the demonstration stage to industrial-scale production. One energy expert likened the process to roasting one turkey, then having to roast one thousand turkeys, making sure they are not burnt on the outside nor undercooked on the inside, and then continuously roasting 100,000 turkeys, each of them having to turn out perfectly crispy and good. Many biofuel projects are currently at the one thousand-turkey stage.

Biofuel is not expected to be cheaper than oil and may even need subsidies from consumers. Most types of biofuel are not economically feasible at this time.

Remember, Professor Hall says a sustainable society needs a minimum EROI of 3:1.

The EROI of biofuel is very low—less than 2:1. It does not create enough excess energy to maintain a functioning society.

Although making biofuel is challenging, we are in favor of using it to produce jet fuel. But for everything else, why focus on biofuels when instead we can save consumers money by using geothermal?

Iceland and geothermal

Like the Big Island, Iceland is a volcanic island with a geothermal resource.

Unlike Hawai'i, though, Iceland has managed to make itself energy- and food-secure.

In fact, electricity costs in Iceland are half of ours. And Iceland exports its cheap electricity in the form of aluminum. That provides its people with hard currency to buy food, which they have a hard time growing there.

Here's something straightforward that Iceland learned and put into practice that we in Hawai'i have not: cheap and proven technology, and clean energy projects, protect an economy from oil crises.

A few years back, I visited Iceland as a guest of Reyjkavik Geothermal. I was very interested to see what they're doing there. I wanted to learn how Iceland went from being a developing country in the 1970s to one of the most productive countries in the world. I was curious to see how they are leveraging geothermal energy.

I learned that the country is totally free of oil for electrical generation. It uses geothermal and hydroelectric energy, resulting in electricity that costs its residents the equivalent of sixteen cents per kilowatt-hour in 2020. As a comparison, here in Hawai'i County in mid-2020, we paid more than twice that much for residential electricity use: thirty-six cents per kilowatt-hour.

Because Iceland chose a proven, low-cost technology as the foundation of its energy program, it's competitive with the rest of the world and now has a high standard of living, despite the country having gone through a severe bank meltdown in 2008.

Everybody knows that Iceland's economy crashed in 2008. That happened because the country privatized its banking industry, the banks went crazy, and the economy got caught in the downturn. So while it's true that the 2008 economic downturn hit Iceland especially hard, that was due to financial matters, not energy ones.

It's because the country has cheap energy that it managed to successfully pull out of that recession and recover from its banks' excesses. Between fishing, geothermal, and hydroelectric, they have food and fuel in abundance.

It shows us that if you're in a competitive position relative to energy, and don't do anything stupid, you can withstand any oil-induced depression or recession.

When we arrived in Iceland, we took a cab into Reykjavik and my first observation was that there are hardly any trees there. The lava base was very familiar to those of us who live on Big Island's east side. I also noticed there are no overhead electric lines. Everything is underground.

On our way into town, we passed an aluminum manufacturing company. I expected it to be belching black smoke, but there wasn't even a wisp of steam. It looked totally benign.

In Reykjavik, we got a car and drove to the Blue Lagoon. That's a popular geothermal spa located in a lava field adjacent to a geothermal power station, which supplies the hot water.

At the nearby geothermal plant, there were steam plumes going into the air. (Iceland and the Philippines both allow some direct venting into the atmosphere that Hawai'i does not.)

To understand the distance, here's a comparison: If KTA Pu'ainako was the Blue Lagoon, the geothermal plant was perhaps as far away as the Prince Kuhio Shopping Center—maybe a quarter-mile away.

The Blue Lagoon's warm seawater stays around 102 degrees Fahrenheit year-round and is rich in minerals. People relaxing in the huge lagoon rubbed very fine silica mud on their faces for its therapeutic value. It felt kind of good. The water smelled slightly of sulfur and tasted a little salty. It flowed in continuously, and I could open my eyes underwater.

It's an extremely popular place to visit. In 2018, 1.3 million people visited, paid a hefty entrance fee, and leisurely soaked in the Blue Lagoon.

Clearly, it's safe (and popular) to bathe in the hot mineral water that's heated by the adjacent geothermal plant. Icelandic citizens are among the world's most educated and they also have a very high voting rate—around 80 percent. They must know something we don't.

It makes me think about triple rinsing, a concept I know from farming. We farmers understand that "the dose makes the poison." For instance, the instructions for disposing of any chemical container, even the most toxic, is to triple rinse it before disposal. The idea is that if some unsuspecting person grabs the container and uses it for drinking water, it won't hurt them. It seemed to me that the geothermal plant's emissions are diluted by the air, much like triple rinsing.

We had coffee with the Reykjavik Geothermal project manager, David Stefansson, and his wife Olga Fedorova, who's an international trade lawyer and Russian translator. We learned a lot about Iceland's history and its move from coal to geothermal many years ago. We learned that the island's trees were cut down for fuel long ago.

It was easy to see that Iceland has inoculated itself from rising oil prices. Its economy depends on cheap energy and fishing as its base. The country's tourism also increased when it devalued its currency, so cheap energy had an additional benefit.

The country has made itself food-secure because its geothermal electricity is cheap relative to using other energy sources. As long as Iceland's electricity costs are lower than its competitors', when the country exports its electricity-intensive aluminum, for instance, it will always have money coming into the economy.

Iceland is concerned about its dependence on fossil fuels for transportation. It has a commercial hydrogen refueling station, and I rode in an SUV powered by methane from municipal waste. They are even looking into making liquid fuels from geothermal electricity and carbon dioxide.

Visiting Iceland was like touring a lab. It was interesting to see how a native people has coped so well. You go over there and look around and say, "Holy smokes! It can be done."

I'd like to learn more about the leaders who forced the change and made Icelanders among the most prosperous people in the world. Now to do it here.

Geothermal energy in the Philippines: 100 percent dependable

When former Big Island Mayor Billy Kenoi was in office, he declared that geothermal should be the Big Island's primary source of base power. He was a strong champion of geothermal. He had guts.

The Philippines, which lies alongside the Pacific Ring of Fire, is the second-largest geothermal producer in the world. The country plans to generate more than 500 gigawatt-hours of electricity by the end of 2030 and is well on its way.

Billy Kenoi signed a sister-city relationship with Ormoc City, Philippines, and led a delegation there, which I joined. Ormoc City is similar to the Big Island in both population size and economy. When we visited in 2012, it was generating more than 700 megawatts of electrical power from geothermal. The Big Island was generating only 30 megawatts.

I asked the manager of the primary geothermal developer there, Energy Development Corporation (EDC), how dependable they are in providing power. He told me they'd had zero dependability issues over the years.

We visited the EDC geothermal production site, which generated the 700 megawatts of electricity for the Ormoc City area. They have geothermal projects in other locations, as well. We toured the Tongonan geothermal field in Leyte, which had a plant capacity of 112 megawatts. It consisted of seventeen production wells and seven reinjection wells.

When we learned the plant sits atop a volcano, the question came up immediately: What about on the flanks of Maunakea? The Philippines is getting geothermal energy from a volcano that last erupted 100,000 years ago. Could we do the same from one that erupted four thousand years ago, such as Maunakea?

The EDC is impressive not only because of its years of experience but also because of the social and environmental component of its business philosophy. It works with the surrounding communities in many areas of mutual benefit — from tax credits to schooling, reforestation, and more. Every plant has a nurse on site. The organization is extremely safety conscious.

It's a company that knows what it's doing. They have a lot of expertise in steam-field geothermal, the kind that would be most applicable in Hawai'i.

Using this stable, low-cost, and proven technology resource will pay enormous dividends to Philippines society in the future. It's clear that as the price of oil rises and they bring more geothermal online, individual Filipinos will see their standard of living rise. If we in Hawai'i took similar bold steps, our standard of living would also rise.

We learned they had a ten-year deal in which the geothermal company built the plant and then the Filipino people bought it back.

By the time we got to the Philippines to see the operation, everybody there—from the folks who swept the floors to the highest executive—was Filipino. Every single employee. And they own the facility.

Can you imagine if the Department of Hawaiian Home Lands did the same thing, and the Hawaiian people owned and ran the geothermal facility?

Here's something else that could happen. You'd have a geothermal facility on the side of a volcano, on Hawaiian Home Lands, in a cold climate zone where you could grow all kinds of temperate crops—apples, oranges, peaches, nectarines, grapes, and more. All you'd need is water. And if you owned the power source, you could give your people a break on electricity costs. So all of a sudden, they'd be doing whatever they wanted to do—manufacturing or producing or whatever.

There are a lot of advantages to moving in that direction and the question becomes, "So why is nobody advocating for geothermal?"

The answer is that there's only one geothermal company. There are many solar companies and organizations that are constantly at the legislature advocating for their projects. But nobody's advocating for geothermal like that.

If the Hawaiian Home Lands people wanted it, all they'd have to do is demand it happen and it would get done. They just have to take the first steps and make it happen.

As we go forward and see what happens with geothermal and other energy projects, the maka'āinana (rubbah slippah folks) will see who our real leaders are. Who's looking after our best interests instead of their own?

Who are today's leaders?

To those who think they are today's Hawaiian leaders—who aspire to be ali'i as they point their fingers in the air and pronounce what we must do to preserve the past—don't forget the rest of us. The rubbah slippah folks.

I don't see you leading us forward, but only backward. You want to keep everything the way it used to be while we march straight ahead into crisis.

You who want to be leaders and are fighting against the geothermal energy that will help our people, remember this: "You cannot be ali'i if you cannot feed the people."

How is trying to shut down our geothermal resource (which will substantially reduce our electricity costs), outlaw our biotech options (which will dramatically reduce food costs), and keep out the TMT (which will open up all sorts of new opportunities) helping our people?

Our world is changing. There's more and more homelessness here on this island. More than half of all Hawaiians no longer live in Hawai'i. Young folks cannot find jobs. Farmers keep getting older because young people are not going into farming.

What will happen to the rubbah slippah folks in the face of finite resources?

- Geothermal is a gift from Pele that will protect us from electricity and other costs that are spiraling out of control. Why would anyone aspiring to be ali'i want to take away this gift in the face of declining resources?

- Biotechnology is a tool that will help us safely feed our people. Why would anyone aspiring to be ali'i take this tool away from the farmers who are trying to feed people? The farmers representing 90 percent of all farm sales on the Big Island favor using biotech tools. Why look to outsiders for advice when Big Island farmers are telling you what you need to know?

- The TMT brings our young people great opportunity and inspiration, and it brings the island economic gain, jobs, and more than $50 million in cash for the education of our keiki. Why would anyone aspiring to be ali'i take these opportunities away from our future generations?

Ke Kānāwai Māmalahoe, or The Law of the Splintered Paddle, was proclaimed by the chief Kamehameha in 1797. It talks about the responsibility chiefs have to serve, care for, and take responsibility for one's people. It's widely accepted that the edict was not something Kamehameha came up with but had already existed in Hawai'i for generations. It still does, as it's now written into the Hawai'i's state constitution. It says, basically, that rubbah slippah folks have the right to disagree with (self-proclaimed) ali'i if those "ali'i" don't take care of them. Take note.

Also: If Hawaiians didn't do or use something in pre-Western-contact times, it's bad? Is that truly your thinking?

Would Kamehameha or Kalākaua or Lili'uokalani agree?

Chapter 15

Rethinking Our Electrical Utility

You know how I first became so concerned about rising electricity costs here on the Big Island? It's because I'm always looking five, ten, and twenty years down the road to see how what we're doing right now will affect our children and grandchildren.

Our expensive electricity, of course, impacts so many aspects of our lives—what we eat, what we buy, how we travel, and how much it all costs.

And turning on a light has an effect far beyond your home. When we pay our electricity bills, our dollars travel from Hilo to Honolulu and then get sent to shareholders, many of them not in Hawai'i. That money doesn't recirculate here on the island and it doesn't benefit our local economy.

I wrote about rising electricity costs when I talked about peak oil, but I didn't mention a possibility that came up and why we tried so hard to make it happen.

In 2015, it looked like Hawaiian Electric Industries (HEI), the parent company of Hawaiian Electric Company (HECO), was going to be sold for $4.3 billion to Florida-based NextEra Energy, which calls itself the world's largest utility company.

It was an excellent time to think about alternatives.

HECO had been having a tough time making the kind of changes Hawai'i needs. HECO is located on O'ahu, but it makes all the decisions regarding electricity here on Hawai'i Island—and it isn't clear their decisions are always in our best interest.

As ratepayers, our best interest is inexpensive electricity so we can keep our lights on. HECO's primary interest is making sure its shareholders get good returns on their investments.

O'ahu has a serious electricity problem. The island has no proven technology base power alternative to fossil fuels. It also has limited opportunities to integrate solar and wind powers.

I can see why HECO decided biofuels would have to be a solution for O'ahu. I can even understand why they changed their minds and decided to bring on more photovoltaic (PV) solar. They do need everything!

But what I couldn't understand is why HECO tried to force the Big Island to go that same route. HECO was offering subsidies to farmers and ranchers for producing biofuel materials.

I started worrying that would prevent us on the Big Island from using our best resource, geothermal, which we know is the cheapest electricity source and will be available to us for millennia. Not only is it inexpensive, but as I mentioned, geothermal is the only renewable energy source that can pay royalties back to Hawaiians.

Every island is different. Our island has the lowest median family income of all the Hawaiian Islands. It's those folks on the lowest rung of the economic ladder whose lights get turned off first when they can't pay the bill. Going down that road—the one where costs are so high that people can't afford to pay their power bill—separates us into haves and have-nots. It rigs the game in favor of those who have money. That will absolutely tear our society apart.

We on the Big Island need a different strategy—one that focuses on our island's unique resources and environment.

NextEra's plan for Hawai'i was to use utility-scale solar, backed up by liquefied natural gas (LNG) as a bridge fuel. Some of us, though, knew that the average shale oil and gas well lasts only about four years. We were very concerned about the model that relies on LNG and its impact on Big Island ratepayers.

We also knew there is plenty of geothermal activity on this island we could use in place of LNG. There were (and still are) options.

When we learned we might end up with NextEra, and heard about its plans, we wanted a seat at that table. Instead of letting Hawai'i Island be negatively affected by that merger, we wondered if this island could have a different ownership model for its energy services.

How would we achieve that? A group of us decided to put together a business model that helped us maximize value to the people.

We brought together several community grassroots organizations and together we asked the Kaua'i Island Utility Cooperative (KIUC) folks to come to Hilo and brief us on how they formed Kaua'i's nonprofit, community-based electric utility. We knew that having such a utility cooperative here on the Big Island would give us more control over our future.

Electric co-ops in this country started back in the Roosevelt era, when farmers and ranchers each put $5 into a cooperative to bring electricity to their rural areas. Not-for-profit electric co-ops align with how we think and live here in Hawai'i. Members elect local directors to represent them. Co-ops work with other co-ops—they cooperate—on financing and research, help each other after storms, and assist at other times as needed. Profits go back to the co-op's members.

As of October 2021, cooperatives power 56 percent of the nation's landmass. They own and maintain 2.7 million miles of line—that's 42 percent of all U.S. electric distribution lines. They serve 42 million people across more than 2,500 counties and power more than 20 million businesses, homes, schools, and farms in 48 states.

In 2019, America's electricity co-ops returned more than $1.3 billion in capital credits to their members.

So how did Kaua'i end up with an electric co-op? It was amazing to hear what KIUC went through to purchase Kaua'i Electric Company and form its utility cooperative.

In 1999, Citizens Utilities Company, which owned Kaua'i Electric, announced it was selling the utility. A group quickly gathered and put together a bid to purchase the electric company.

Initially, Kaua'i's mayor and county council were against the purchase. The public utility commission (PUC) turned down KIUC's first purchase bid as not being in the best interest of users.

But the founding group reworked its plan and presented another bid. That time, it was successful.

In total, it took about two years for them to purchase Kaua'i Electric Company, which it did in 2002 for $215 million. At the time of purchase, KIUC had nearly $100 million in retained earnings that would otherwise have gone off-island but instead stayed in the state.

And the county administrators that were originally against the purchase? One of the KIUC board members told us, "They're all on board now."

We learned that on Kaua'i, every person or entity with an electric meter gets one vote. Those votes elect the nine-member board of directors that guides the co-op's direction.

Because the people select its board, the co-op's organization reflects what the people of Kaua'i want. It takes into account both community concerns and local perspectives of aloha 'āina. It also allows the co-op to respond to changes quickly. That's especially important now because declining natural resources require being agile, flexible, and strategic.

At first, we learned, there was almost complete, and repeated, board turnover as the ratepayers kept voting out board members who weren't doing what they wanted. Over time, though, the board stabilized.

Since 2003, Kauai's electricity users have received tens of millions of dollars in direct refunds and patronage capital—the amount of money left over after the bills are all paid and the co-op has met its lenders' requirements. That money circulates back into the local community.

A national co-op financing association helps KIUC fund projects, which results in much lower financing costs. I visited the national headquarters of the National Rural Utilities Cooperative Finance Corporation (CFC) in Virginia and learned it's a strong national association made up of 900 utility co-ops, and exists to help its members. In October 2020, it had more than $28 billion in assets. Because it's a nonprofit, it pays no taxes.

When I met with its senior staff, I briefed them about the preparations we were making in case an opportunity arose to purchase the Big Island's Hawaii Electric Light Company (HELCO) and convert it to an energy cooperative.

They told me that their resources were at our disposal.

It was eye-opening to understand that we wouldn't be alone. I realized we would not be a small, stand-alone utility co-op but one of 900 in the nation. We would be able to call upon incredible technical expertise—exponentially more than what we would otherwise have access to as a stand-alone co-op out in the middle of the Pacific.

A co-op can be a terrific solution if conditions are right.

Forming the Hawai'i Island Energy Cooperative

In January 2015, a steering committee of Big Island community members applied to the PUC to form the Hawai'i Island Energy Cooperative (HIEC).

HIEC is "a non-profit cooperative association formed by community and business leaders on Hawai'i Island to explore the potential merits of a community-based, cooperative ownership structure for electric utility service on the Big Island. HIEC is also exploring how other energy sectors, such as transportation, can be transformed to be more sustainable and environmentally friendly."

A co-op considers multiple energy issues. Not only electricity but also ground transportation, fertilizer, and food, which is why it's called the Hawai'i Island Energy Co-op as opposed to "Electricity Co-op." We take a broader view.

An investor-owned utility model is not necessarily bad, but we wanted to look at homegrown alternatives that would allow us to turn to power sources—renewable, environmentally friendly, and cost-effective ones—that suit us best.

We knew our HIEC model, with its local control, would help us adapt more quickly to future situations we couldn't yet anticipate. The co-op model would also help us become more competitive with the rest of the world without leaving anyone behind.

As a co-op, we would be in control of our direction and our destiny. We would manage it ourselves, instead of being dependent on people whose end goal was trying to make a dollar for investors.

HELCO, the Big Island subsidiary of HEI, was not for sale when we formed HIEC, so we didn't submit an offer to purchase it. But we wanted to be ready in case the opportunity to buy it arose. We wanted to position our co-op as an option worthy of consideration, one that would take Hawai'i Island in a different and stronger energy direction.

Much community support for HIEC

Also in September 2015, a *Honolulu Civil Beat* reporter interviewed some of more than forty elected officials committed to exploring the potential of public utilities. As the merger deal between NextEra and Hawaiian Electric was being discussed, those officials wanted more options.

"Public utilities don't need higher rates to make profits for shareholders, and as a result, they tend to have significantly lower rates than for-profit utilities across the country," said State Rep. Chris Lee, who headed the House Energy and Environment Committee, a standing committee of the Hawai'i House of Representatives.

House Minority Leader Beth Fukumoto Chang and fellow Republican Representative Cynthia Thielen also said the public utility option should be explored.

"As Republicans and Democrats, we have differences," Fukumoto said. "But we can all agree that the skyrocketing cost of electricity is detrimental to local families. Until NextEra provides a framework for customer savings, it would be irresponsible not to explore options like co-ops and other alternatives."

Around that same time, I spoke on a League of Women Voters forum. I told the moderator, Pearl Johnson, that we were adopting the Wayne Gretsky strategy. The Canadian ice hockey player Gretsky says you skate to where the puck is going to be, not where it already is.

His quote refers, of course, to planning ahead and it's a great example of insightful leadership. It's something I learned from my Pop, too, in so many ways.

We decided to prepare our co-op option in case an opportunity arose. If we waited to start putting together our co-op until an opportunity came up, it would have been too late.

I spoke at a Maui Energy Conference where the moderator asked: "Imagine it's 2045, and Hawai'i is a wonderful place because we're using 100 percent renewable energy. How did we get here?"

I talked about the Hawaii Island Energy Cooperative as being straightforward:

- It saves money.
- It's a nonprofit, and all the profits that would otherwise go to shareholders go, instead, to the folks with electric meters.
- It's predictable. Everything else that happens with energy between now and 2045 is unpredictable. But saving money due to your business model would be predictable.

The moderator emphasized, for the audience outside Hawai'i, that it's Hawaiian-style to prepare in advance. People can't just come in and look at the balance sheets, say they're going to invest here, and then expect changes to happen quickly.

That's true. Things work differently here. Hawai'i's culture has evolved from a society where relationships were reciprocal, where the more you gave, the more you got back, into a market economy that's more along the lines of "the more you get, the more you get." There is a lingering, uncomfortable feeling that the capitalist system is suspect.

I think that's part of the reason Hawaiians introduce themselves by talking about who they are and mention some of their genealogy. We want to know who we're talking to, who we're dealing with.

You don't come in here all of a sudden and try to rush things through on us. That doesn't work here.

We need to control our direction to take care of ourselves, and even more importantly, so our kids and grandkids and their grandkids will be able to adapt to changing conditions and take care of themselves. The future is not going to look or work like it always has, and we need to be doing our long-term planning now.

It's like my Pop taught me—plan for the future by taking small steps now, and you won't have to take drastic, catastrophic measures just to survive.

Those survival lessons I learned from my Pop were simple, and it was time to put them into play.

The steering committee we created to form HIEC was our way of skating to where the puck will be, or climbing the bamboo pole. We did all the legwork, research, and information-gathering to be ready if there is an opportunity. We were planning ahead.

Here are the goals and benefits of a Hawai'i Island Energy Cooperative:

- Local, democratic control over one of the most important infrastructures and public utilities on the island. That would provide more benefits to island residents, with all profits staying here at home.

- A focus on community over off-island, corporate shareholder priorities, as the cooperative would work for sustainable development of the island's communities through approved and accepted policies by its members.

- Lower electric costs through greater efforts to develop island-based energy sources and improve energy efficiency, as well as accelerated adoption of smart grid technologies.

- Greater overall energy independence and sustainability through a comprehensive and integrated approach to all energy-consuming sectors on the island.

- Development of island-produced fuels to provide an energy source for both electricity generation and transportation.

The Big Island has a huge advantage in working to achieve 100 percent renewable energy. The island's renewable energy sales were at 34.7 percent in 2019 and 43.4 percent in 2020, according to HECO.

The gradual return of Puna Geothermal Venture, which came back online in November 2020 (after having shut down in May 2018 due to the Kīlauea eruption), will play a larger role in 2021.

HECO predicts the Big Island could get to more than 90 percent renewables by 2030. It appears that we can probably avoid using LNG entirely.

Ultimately, the NextEra/Hawaiian Electric deal was not approved and didn't happen. If it had, your dollars would have journeyed even farther offshore, been diverted through NextEra's headquarters in Florida, and then flown off to line the pockets of global investors.

Compare that to what happens on Kaua'i: when a resident there flips a light switch, their dollars flow back to the community utility, KIUC, which uses the money to operate the system. And when KIUC has more than it needs, it sends the profits sent right back into the pockets of Kaua'i ratepayers.

Although HIEC didn't ultimately get the opportunity to purchase the Big Island's electric utility, starting the process when we did was the right thing to do.

Today, it has evolved into Sustainable Energy Hawaii (SEH).

We changed the name in May 2020 when we participated in the PUC docket on HELCO and Puna Geothermal Venture. With the same values we continue advocating for improved energy strategies for the island.

I am currently the SEH president, although I will step aside and let someone else lead the way in due time. Noel Morin is SEH's vice chairman, Peter Sternlicht is treasurer, and Noelani Kalipi is secretary. Directors are Jerry Chang, Dave De Luz, Jr., and Kanani Aton.

Chapter 16

Sustainability and the Future

In January 2016, we decided to close the farm. The bananas we were bagging would be our last harvest. They'd be ready in March.

It was a coincidence that on the same day we announced we were closing, Alexander & Baldwin—Hawai'i's last surviving sugar plantation, which had started in 1869 and still had a 36,000-acre sugar plantation on Maui—announced it was transitioning out of sugar.

Its Executive Chairman Stanley M. Kuriyama said, "The roughly $30 million agribusiness operating loss we expect to incur in 2015, and the forecast for continued significant losses, clearly are not sustainable, and we must now move forward with a new concept for our lands that allows us to keep them in productive agricultural use."

We understood that completely. "Transitioning" was the right word for us, too.

We didn't know exactly what our transition would look like, but I knew we'd still be around. For starters, a dairy that was already leasing land to grow corn for its cows was going to lease our banana land to plant more.

I told our workers that we did have an option. The state had just opened up bids for the very first medical marijuana licenses, and a group wanting to apply for a license had approached me. They wanted to lease some of our land as well as our hydroelectric plant and try for one of those licenses.

We were already working on shutting down the farm when that group approached me, and at first I wasn't sure how I felt about it. I considered the idea and then said I would only lease to them if they agreed to consider my workers for jobs first. They said they would.

I also made some conditions regarding security. There was no guarantee, of course, that their bid for a medical marijuana license would be successful. Still, on the outside chance it was, they would have to take care of the community—especially in terms of security—so I could ensure that our neighbors felt safe. They agreed to this, too.

They asked me to participate with their group because they realized I know what I'm talking about when it comes to growing things and also about energy.

I asked my workers if they wanted to be considered for jobs with the medical marijuana company, and it turned out that all of them did. That was significant to me. One of our workers had worked for us for thirty-eight years, and another for twenty-three.

It was never just about me, but it was about all of us. I wrote earlier about how I learned in Vietnam—and continue to believe—that either we all came home or no one came home. Once I knew my employees wanted to work there, I knew I'd do whatever I could to help the group win that medical marijuana license because it meant I was helping my workers get jobs.

At the same time, I started learning everything I could about the medical use of cannabis and realized how vast and important its potential is for genuinely helping people.

Here in Hawai'i, one of my inspirations was Jari Sugano and her young daughter MJ, who was six years old at the time. MJ has a rare disorder that causes her to have uncontrollable seizures. Medical cannabis is one of the only medications that helps her.

I realized our Daniel K. Inouye College of Pharmacy at UH Hilo could potentially lead the way in medical cannabis research, and our college of agriculture could spearhead production methods. It all seemed really positive to me. It still does.

Our last banana harvest

We did something different for our final banana harvest. Instead of leaving the tall banana bunches as we harvested, we used cane knives and chopped them down. So by the time we got to the last bananas, all the bunches were down. Two or three weeks later, we had farmers in there preparing the land for their crops.

We didn't have to cut down the banana bunches like that. We could have just left them, because the lease read "as-is." But doing that let us keep our people employed as long as possible.

They wanted to work until the last day, instead of leaving and relying on unemployment. They were willing to work, and, shoot, you want to work? I'll pay you.

We did a lot of work we could have left for the next farmers to do, but I did that deliberately. I did it both to employ my workers for as long as possible and also to make it easier for new farmers to come in. It meant there was less material that needed to deteriorate. It was about getting to the point that when we transition to rotating crops, it's continuous.

Full circle, but not the end.

We decided to give away our last banana harvest instead of selling them.

We let the public know, and then one Friday morning in March, we set up tables at the Hilo soccer fields where people could drive in, park easily, and pick some up. It was a wonderful day, and we were happy to be able to thank the community for its thirty-five years of support. We gave away three hundred boxes of bananas.

On April 29, 2016, we stood around in the Hamakua Springs office waiting to learn if we were one of two Big Island groups that would be granted a medical cannabis dispensary license. They were going to announce it at 11:30 that morning.

We'd already closed down the farm, so we were no longer using that office to take orders anymore. But we hung around there anyway, watching the *Hawaii News Now* press conference on five or six iPhones, two or three iPads, and a couple computers.

So that's how we found out, same as everybody else, that our company Lau Ola was awarded one of the Big Island licenses. The other Hawai'i Island company granted a license was Hawaiian Ethos in Waimea.

When they announced our name, it was like we were watching the Super Bowl and our team had just scored a touchdown. I was elated, and then I thought, "Holy Smokes." It's a huge deal and I was thinking about the big picture. We take the responsibility very seriously.

It was such an honor for our company Lau Ola to be awarded one of two dispensary licenses on Hawai'i Island.

Chapter 17

Full Circle

When I look back at our farm's long story of sustainability, I see that we really did come full circle.

When we started out, the plan was to farm and eventually buy land with the money we earned. We didn't have any money when we were getting started, and there wasn't any land available anyway. That was before the sugar plantations shut down and their land became available. But we just kept going, and that was always our objective—to own land.

That goal was what made us adapt along the way and make change happen when we needed to. We made decisions based on getting ourselves into the position we wanted to be in ten years later.

We've always done that and always been comfortable with change, so that's easy for us now. It's who we are. We change to meet conditions and to keep moving toward where we want to end up.

Then the rise in farming costs happened for external reasons, not due to any fault of our own.

We did the best we could for our workers, but as hard as we tried, we knew at some point, to survive, we would have to make more cuts to our employees' pay and benefits and we didn't want to do that. It just wasn't an option to let ourselves get into that situation. That had a lot to do with why we closed the farm.

I always wanted to make sure we were using the soil and land in a sustainable way, so now we lease land to farmers and have them do crop rotations. We want to run one crop, follow it with another crop and then possibly a third, and keep that going.

Once you get into that rotation, it's sustainable. You're not decreasing your soil. You rarely see that in Hawai'i, though, for many reasons. If your business scale isn't big enough, and if your market isn't large enough, you can't rotate your crops.

But I can do that because we own the land. If you're trying to squeeze every last penny out of a deal, it might not be the most efficient move. In the long run, it is, though, because it's sustainable farming.

And now, thirty years later, here we are. We own land, and that was our original goal. And although we shut down the banana operation, we still have a lot going on at the farm. It's not like one day we simply closed and rode off into the sunset.

It wasn't an end, but a transition.

The COVID-19 pandemic and other uncertainties

Before the pandemic, shale oil was already starting to be depleted. But when COVID-19 hit us around March 2020, it took our attention away from our oil problem. The panic became about the global virus. Climate change took second place, and oil moved down into third place.

The effect of oil on our economy is still tremendously important, even though it's not top of mind right now. Even though we aren't talking about those problems as much right now, they're still out there. They didn't go away. They'll be back.

What's happened with oil is that when the pandemic caused economic activity and travel to decline around the world like never before, Saudi Arabia dropped the price of oil, which caused the bottom to drop out of the oil market.

That was good for the customer, regular folks, because suddenly it was cheap to fill up gas tanks and pay electric bills.

Then oil producers agreed to cut production by a certain amount over some time.

While the price of oil has rebounded some we are still in uncertain times, and it's unclear what will happen going forward. If the oil price stays low, it will be harder for renewables like solar and wind to come online, because they are more expensive than oil.

The pandemic has bought us—the regular rubbah slippah folks—some time. How much time, we don't know.

So much has changed and so much is unclear. We thought it would take a year and a half for COVID-19 vaccines to become available, and then everyone would get vaccinated and things would go back to normal.

Instead, amazingly, we got vaccines in just about a year. But people started demonstrating against getting vaccines and wearing masks. We saw a much more contagious variant of the virus start circulating, and then another one, and found ourselves nowhere near back to normal. There are times we've been actually going in the wrong direction again.

How will we take care of ourselves here in Hawai'i?

As in every other situation, my Pop's words apply. It wasn't until I was older that I realized it was street smarts, common sense, or contingency planning—whatever you want to call those survivor skills—that let me make Pop's, "Not, no can!" (*pound the table*) "Can!!" philosophy a part of my life.

It's easy to say and it sounds dramatic. But how do you actually make those words work for you? It's about how you handle short-term decisions.

While you're working toward long-term goals, you're going to have to make short-term decisions all along the way. Making the wrong short-term decisions will hurt you in the long run if it makes you give up any of your core values.

I can tell you for sure that your core values are worth fighting for. If you're street smart, you can figure out how to make the right decisions even with a short-term disadvantage. Sometimes, you just have to press the gas and "run over the dog" for the bigger picture.

In the long run, it's how you stick to your core values that defines you. It's not money or fame. It really isn't.

These are the core values I consider critical.

- Your family is most important.
- Taking care of today's keiki, and the keiki who will live one hundred years from now, is most important.
- Your good friends are most important. (Note that I said "good" friends. I didn't say "bad" friends.)
- Your word is most important.
- Taking care of the most defenseless around you is most important.
- Leaving no one behind is most important.
- Taking care of your community is most important.
- Taking care of the environment is most important.

I have held onto my core values and have been able to reach several of my long-term goals. I'm still working on others.

To me, the most important things are: that you follow your dreams; look for several solutions to every potential problem, and then look for one more, just in case; and don't sacrifice your core values for any reason.

What would our kūpuna (ancestors) do?

They were smart and practical people. How would they use our resources? Would they build the biggest and best telescope in the world right here on the Big Island?

Just like they used the resources on Maunakea, the basalt, to create hard adze tools, would they figure out how to use the island's gift of geothermal energy to take care of their people? Most of the state's electricity needs could be powered by geothermal wells on the Big Island. Rents and royalties would go to Native Hawaiian people, and all of us would benefit from being free from reliance on oil from the Middle East. We'd be the envy of the world if we did that.

We are somebody's ancestors. We need to make smart decisions now to take care of future generations and meet our people's long-term goals.

Not, no can. CAN!

www.ingramcontent.com/pod-product-compliance
Lightning Source LLC
Chambersburg PA
CBHW050123280326
41933CB00010B/1221